The Second Mouse Gets the Cheese

David Moon's Proverbs for Thinking Investors

W. David Moon

Asbury Publishing

Copyright© 2017 by W. David Moon
All rights reserved.

All rights reserved. No part of this book may be reproduced or transmitted in any form or by any means whatsoever without express written permission from the author, except in the case of brief quotations embodied in critical articles and reviews. Please refer all pertinent questions to the publisher.

Book packaged by Eichner | Fukui Design
Illustrations by Harley Schwadron

ISBN: 978-0-9993626-0-0
APID: 0-9993626-0-7

Printed in the United States of America

W. David Moon
www.davidmoon.com

Asbury Publishing
www.asburypublishing.com

To Sien, Wheeler and Bethany, with my love.

Introduction

Benjamin Graham said that the investor's chief problem—and even his worst enemy—is likely to be himself. The most common investor problems result from poor influences, often ones related to emotion. Investing often involves a constant pull between logic and emotion. Thinking investors make mistakes, but reducing the influence of fear, greed, hope or jealousy in your investment decisions will significantly reduce your mistakes.

This book is for the investor who seeks to tilt his pendulum toward the rational approach.

After reviewing hundreds of my own trades over the years, I discovered that more than 65% of my unprofitable investments were the result of unforced errors. That is, mistakes that, in hindsight, were avoidable. A handful of the ideas in this book are lessons I learned from observing the mistakes of others. Most of the ideas, however, were lessons learned from my own mistakes.

There are ten repeating themes throughout this collection, but I hope it isn't obvious. Good advice rarely, if ever, changes, which is why *Wall Street Journal* columnist Jason Zweig once described his job as writing the exact same thing 50 times a year in such a way that neither his readers nor editors realize he is repeating himself.

Zweig disguises his repetition much better than I do, but educators tell us that we are more likely to remember something after being exposed to it multiple times. Perhaps any noticed repetition will be valuable to you.

My investment influences over the years have been many. Garrett Arms is a brilliant, provocative thinker and investment analyst from whom I have learned much. I am fortunate to work with him. In addition to being generous with his time and advice, Wally Weitz has also been the source of many borrowed investment ideas. I thank both him and quarterly securities filings. Bill Rukeyser has been a wonderful example and teacher of the indivisible processes of thinking and writing. He has made me better at both.

As there are few original ideas or thoughts in life, some of these concepts will sound familiar. I have intentionally presented useful ideas from great investors, but any similarities between my actual words and those of someone else are unintentional, unconscious and solely my error.

The subtitle of this collection, "David Moon's proverbs for thinking investors," isn't intended to suggest any biblical wisdom. The word "proverb" literally translates from the Latin word *proverbium* as "words put forward." Each quote is culled from more than three decades of investing and notetaking. I put forward these words in hope they help you become a more thinking investor.

The Second Mouse Gets the Cheese

The second mouse gets the cheese.

P rofiting from even a revolutionary product or idea does not require being its inventor.

When Henry Ford entered the automobile manufacturing business in 1903, there were already more than two dozen companies in the fledgling industry, none of which exist today. In 1992, IBM introduced the Simon, the world's first smartphone, predating any documented use of the word "smartphone" by three years. The Simon made calls, managed your calendar, kept track of your to-do list and ran other apps—a full 15 years before Apple introduced the iPhone. Social media platform Six Degrees, Betamax, MP3 players, the Mosaic web browser and the Internet Shopping Network are just some of the more recent first-to-market technologies that would quickly be overwhelmed by copycats that improved on those early models.

Investors regularly commit significant money and energy into trying to guess what company is going to invent the next big thing. It is much easier and less risky to identify a company that can improve and profitably monetize a technology, product or process—even if someone else invented it.

It's mathematically impossible for a
business to grow 20% annually forever.

Like sex, investing is one of the few activities
in which there is no safety in numbers.

Don't underestimate the ability of a
large company to squash a little one if the large one
wants the business of the smaller one.

Cataclysmic economic events seldom are.

Dismount a drowning horse, even if in midstream.

Beware of anyone proclaiming the "new normal." Economic series tend to revert to their long-term mean.

Never underestimate the laziness of the American consumer. Two words: "bottled water."

Have a written objective and expectation for each of your investments. "To make money" is not satisfactorily specific.

"Pro forma" is a Greek term that means,
"What would have happened if we ignored
some things that actually did happen."

When Big Co. gets into Little Co.'s high-margin
business, it is a bad sign for Little Co.
When Big Co. gets into Little Co.'s low-margin
business, it is a bad sign for Big Co.

Trying to predict the next Google or Amazon
is not a great investment strategy.

The CEO of a 50 billion dollar company tends to
make more money than the CEO of a 30 billion dollar
company, thus providing a powerful incentive for
corporate acquisitions.

Shareholder letters should be written by
the president or chairman, not a PR intern.

Never buy a stock just to get the dividend.

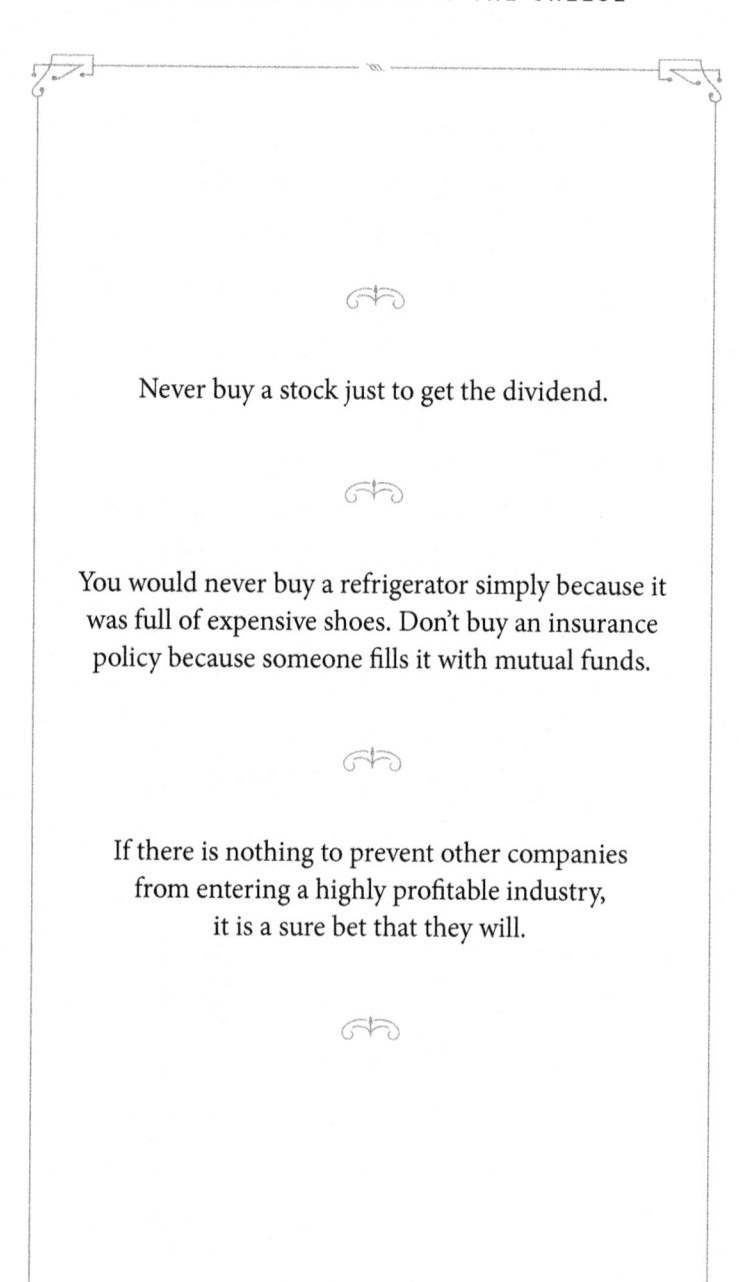

You would never buy a refrigerator simply because it was full of expensive shoes. Don't buy an insurance policy because someone fills it with mutual funds.

If there is nothing to prevent other companies from entering a highly profitable industry, it is a sure bet that they will.

A share of stock represents ownership in a business.
It is not a moving average, Fibonacci line
or candlestick chart.

Interest rates are more important than
you think they are.

Doing nothing is a decision.

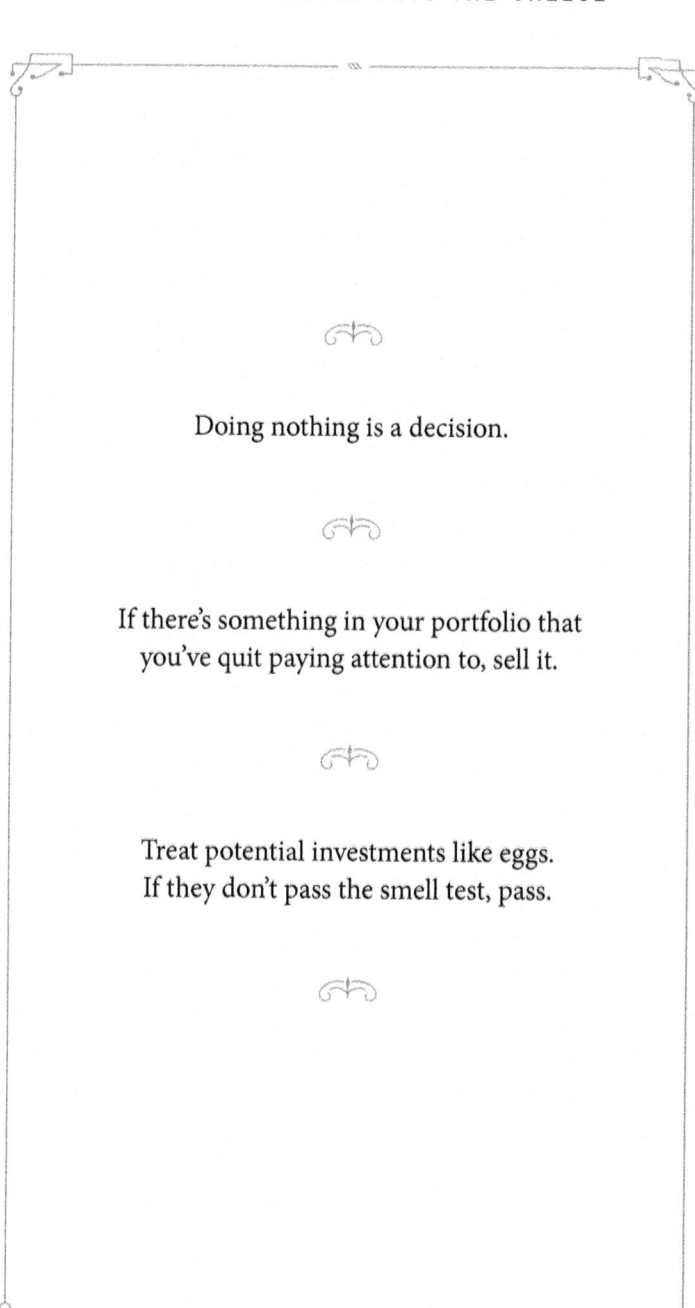

If there's something in your portfolio that
you've quit paying attention to, sell it.

Treat potential investments like eggs.
If they don't pass the smell test, pass.

The ugly dogs are sometimes the best hunters.

In 1962 a 32-year-old hedge fund manager began purchasing shares in the formerly named Valley Falls Company, a Rhode Island textile company founded in 1939. Within only 2 years, the young investor had earned 50% on his investment, and in 1965 he bought the entire company, despite it being in obvious decline. In 1985, the textile company ceased operations.

It was this dwindling business, Berkshire Hathaway, which Warren Buffett used as the investment vehicle that would make him the world's most respected investor. In his trademark folksy, self-deprecating manner, Buffett describes his Berkshire Hathaway purchase as his worst investment of all time. As the business generated operating cash flow for its young owner, Buffett also began selling the company's underutilized mills, which provided even more capital for him to invest in businesses that did have attractive future prospects.

But the entire Berkshire Hathaway empire was built on the foundation of an unpopular, almost discarded business.

Old and boring can be just as profitable as new and exciting when old and boring is available at a bargain price.

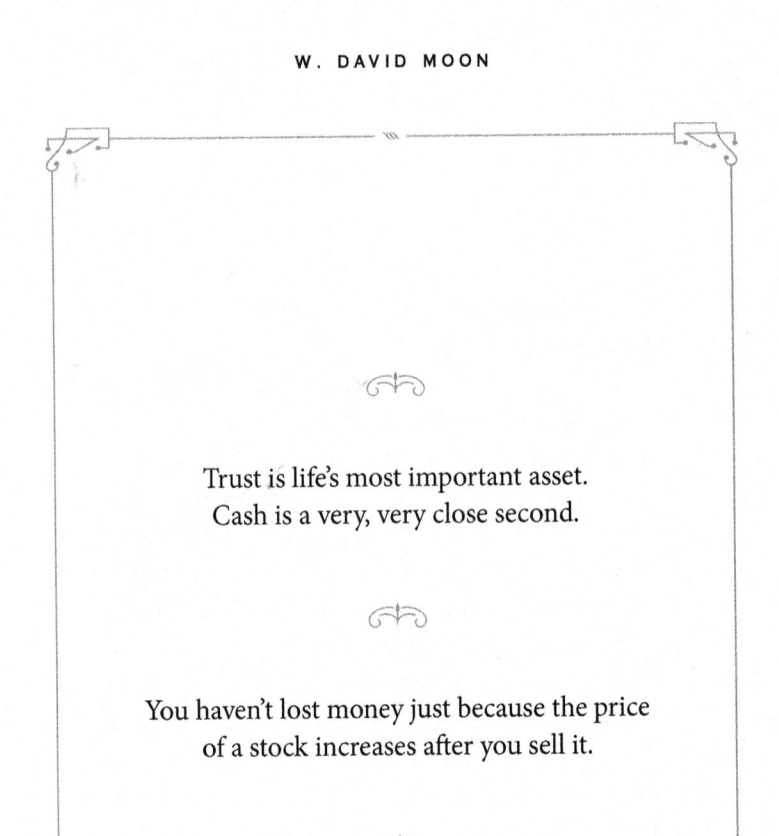

Trust is life's most important asset.
Cash is a very, very close second.

You haven't lost money just because the price
of a stock increases after you sell it.

Don't bet against gravity in the short term or
the U.S. economy in the long term.

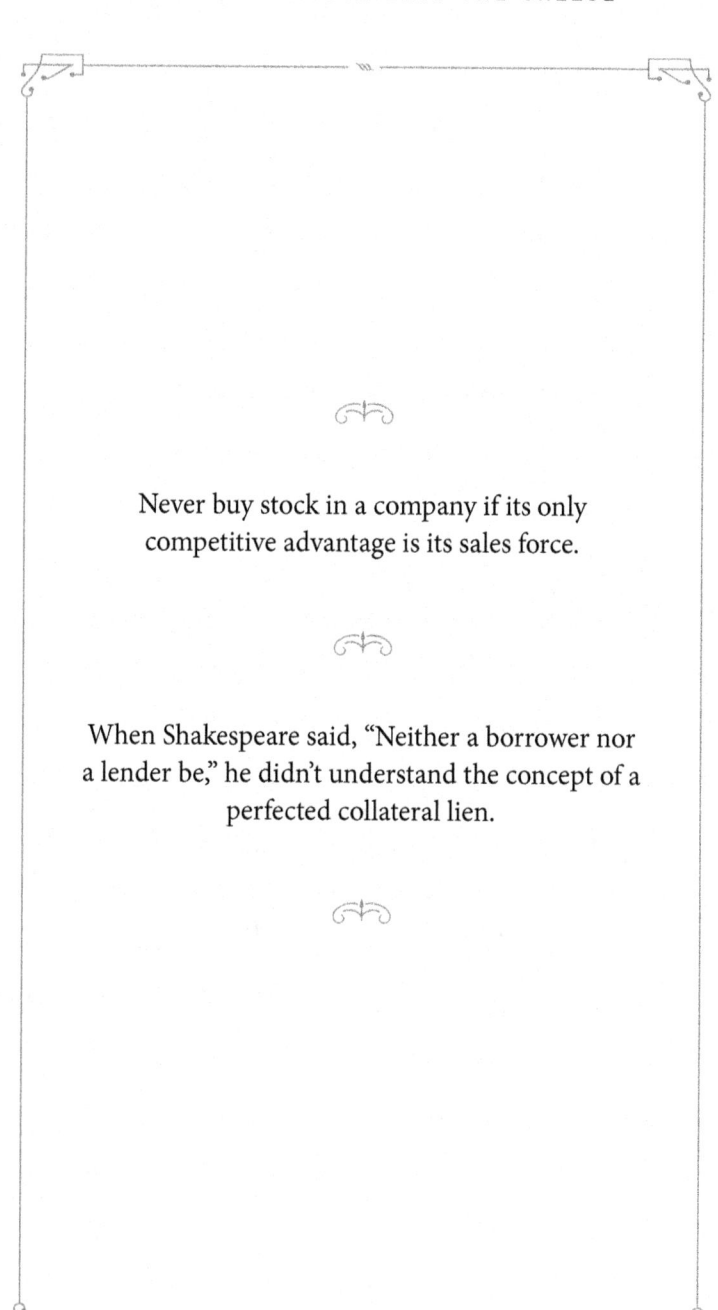

Never buy stock in a company if its only competitive advantage is its sales force.

When Shakespeare said, "Neither a borrower nor a lender be," he didn't understand the concept of a perfected collateral lien.

"Net income" is accountant's fiction.

Predicted synergies from corporate acquisitions are like a politician's campaign promises: easy to offer, difficult to accomplish and often unrealistic.

If it's difficult to determine if a company is in the business of serving customers or generating PR spin, avoid the stock. Or short it.

"Our fourth quarter results fell short of expectations because we didn't expect Christmas on December 25 this year."

If a company repeatedly reports non-recurring items, they aren't non-recurring.

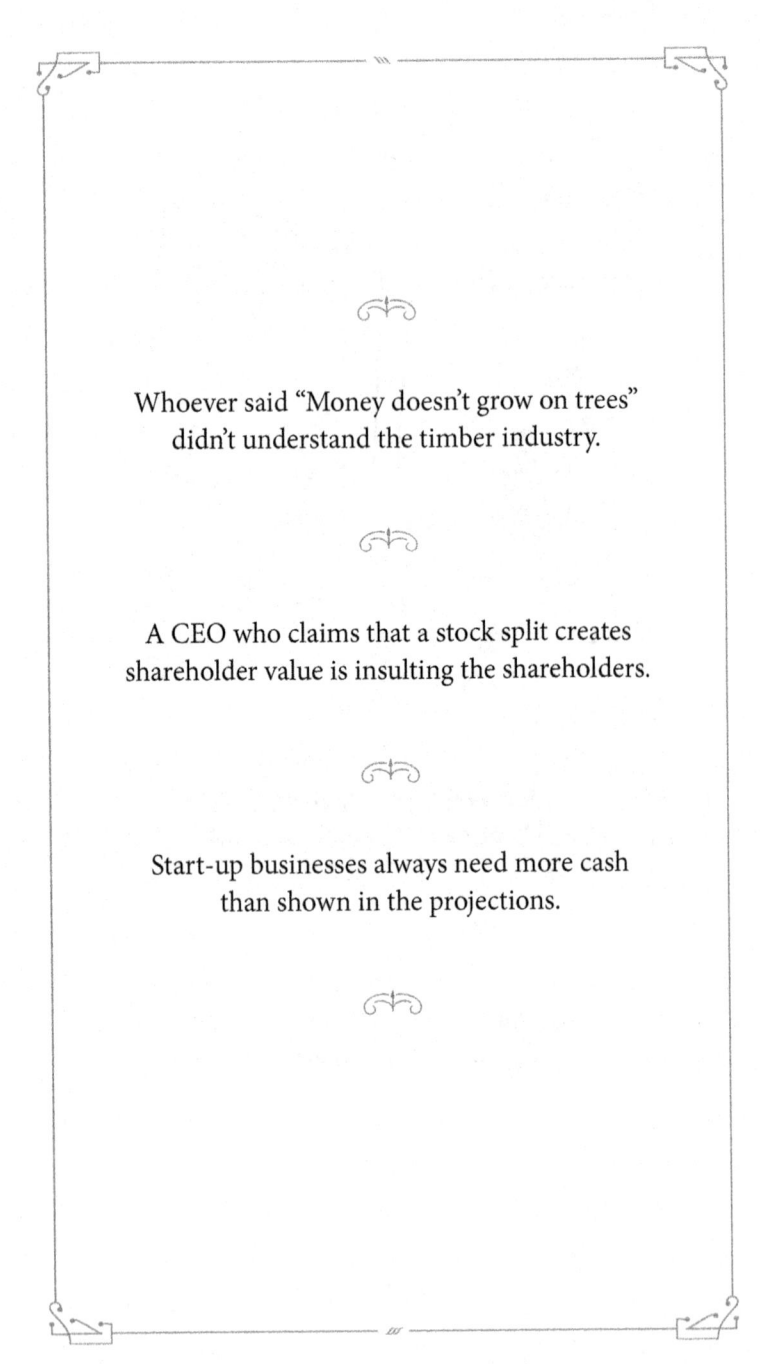

Whoever said "Money doesn't grow on trees" didn't understand the timber industry.

A CEO who claims that a stock split creates shareholder value is insulting the shareholders.

Start-up businesses always need more cash than shown in the projections.

If you don't understand it, don't buy it.

Be wary if a company regularly presents its own definition of income, such as "income excluding expenses we wish we hadn't made" or "income if conditions were different than they are."

A company can make a single quarter's reported earnings be almost anything it would like.

You can make money on a low-growth business if bought at the right price. It is much more difficult to make money investing in a negative-growth business. Time becomes your enemy.

After a company raises all the capital it needs, shareholders become a major nuisance.

Any decent accountant can manipulate net income. Only a crook can manipulate cash.

When a company announces three consecutive
initiatives that have silly acronyms, sell.

Keep a "money journal" where you record things
like investment lessons you learn and
your savings/retirement goals.

Your sunk cost is irrelevant to your next decision.

If a company or mutual fund changes auditors, read
the footnotes to the annual report especially carefully.

Despite how many times you read it, asset allocation is not responsible for 90% of your portfolio's return.

A 1986 paper by Brinson, Hood and Beebower found that 93.6% of the variation between the quarterly returns of two portfolios is explained by the portfolios' asset allocations. Consultants almost immediately began misquoting the findings, claiming that 90% of a portfolio's return is explained by its asset allocation and using the claims to sell their allocation services and systems. Pension plans began hiring consultants offering systems with impressive names like "Tactical Asset Allocation," "Dynamic Allocation" and "Strategic Asset Allocation."

The original study, however, found that asset allocation explained the difference in the returns of two portfolios, not the actual return of either portfolio. That didn't stop financial planners, stockbrokers, banks and investment advisers from misusing the study for marketing purposes. Many of them adopted this false mantra in order to sell market timing systems cleverly disguised and decorated with fancy names and four-color charts.

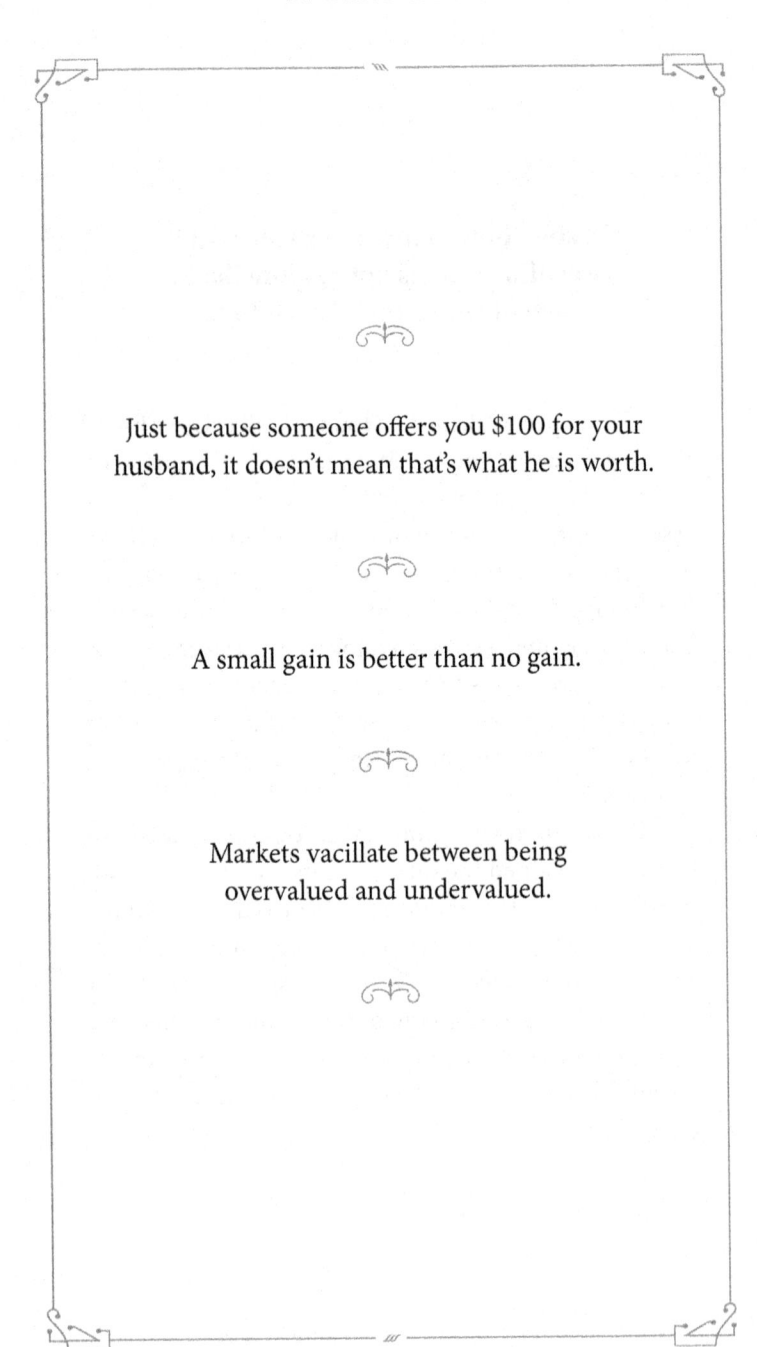

Just because someone offers you $100 for your husband, it doesn't mean that's what he is worth.

A small gain is better than no gain.

Markets vacillate between being overvalued and undervalued.

If you would not buy a security, why hold it?

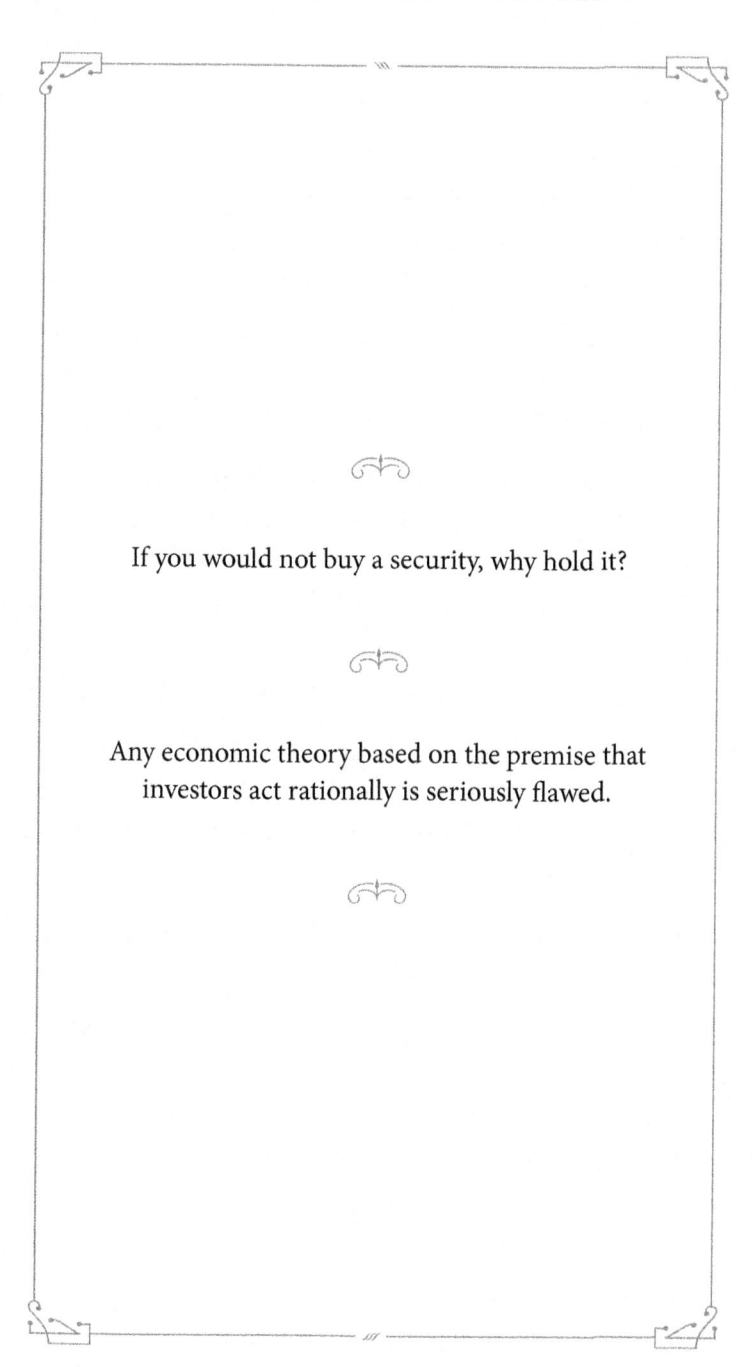

Any economic theory based on the premise that investors act rationally is seriously flawed.

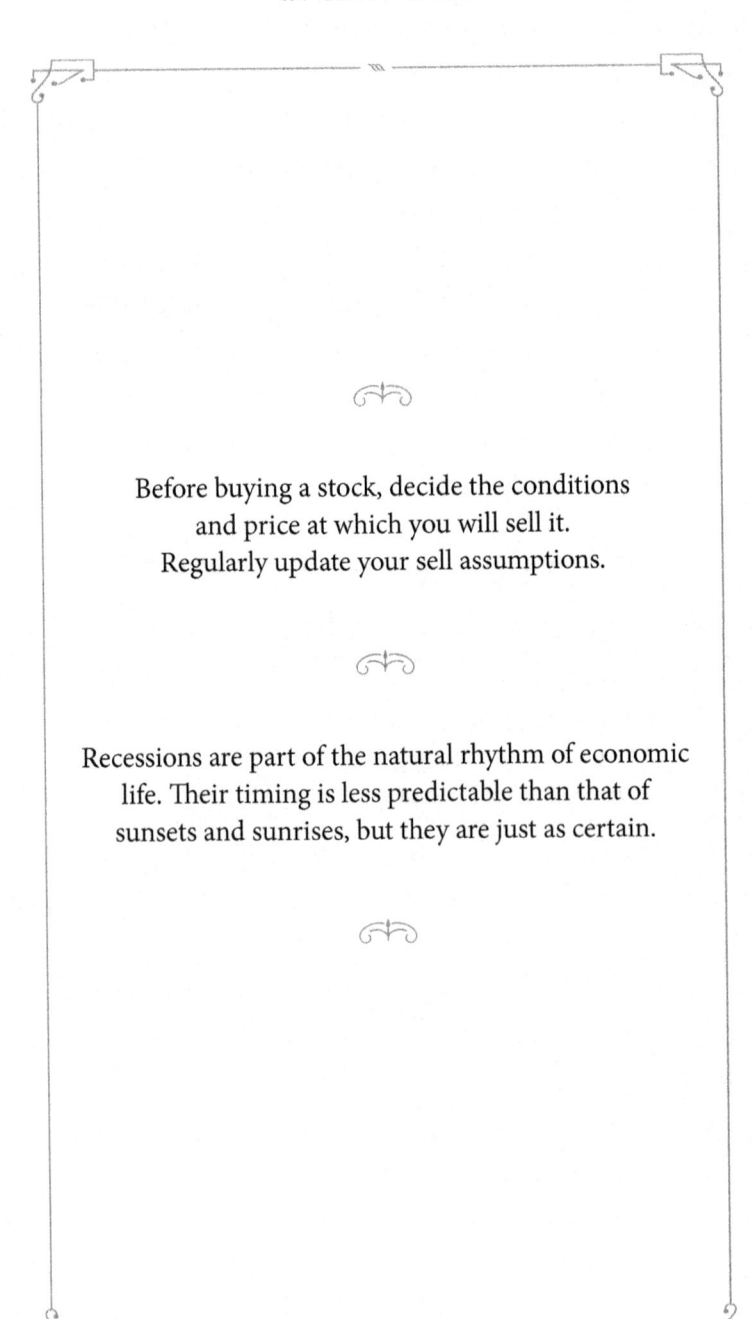

Before buying a stock, decide the conditions
and price at which you will sell it.
Regularly update your sell assumptions.

Recessions are part of the natural rhythm of economic
life. Their timing is less predictable than that of
sunsets and sunrises, but they are just as certain.

A stock split is like cutting your sandwich in half.

Successful investing requires a delicate mix of positive thinking and paranoia. Too much of either guarantees failure.

At the right price, any asset is an attractive investment.

Every asset is worth something. If you want to guarantee that you will eventually lose a lot of money, repeatedly buy assets for more than they are worth.

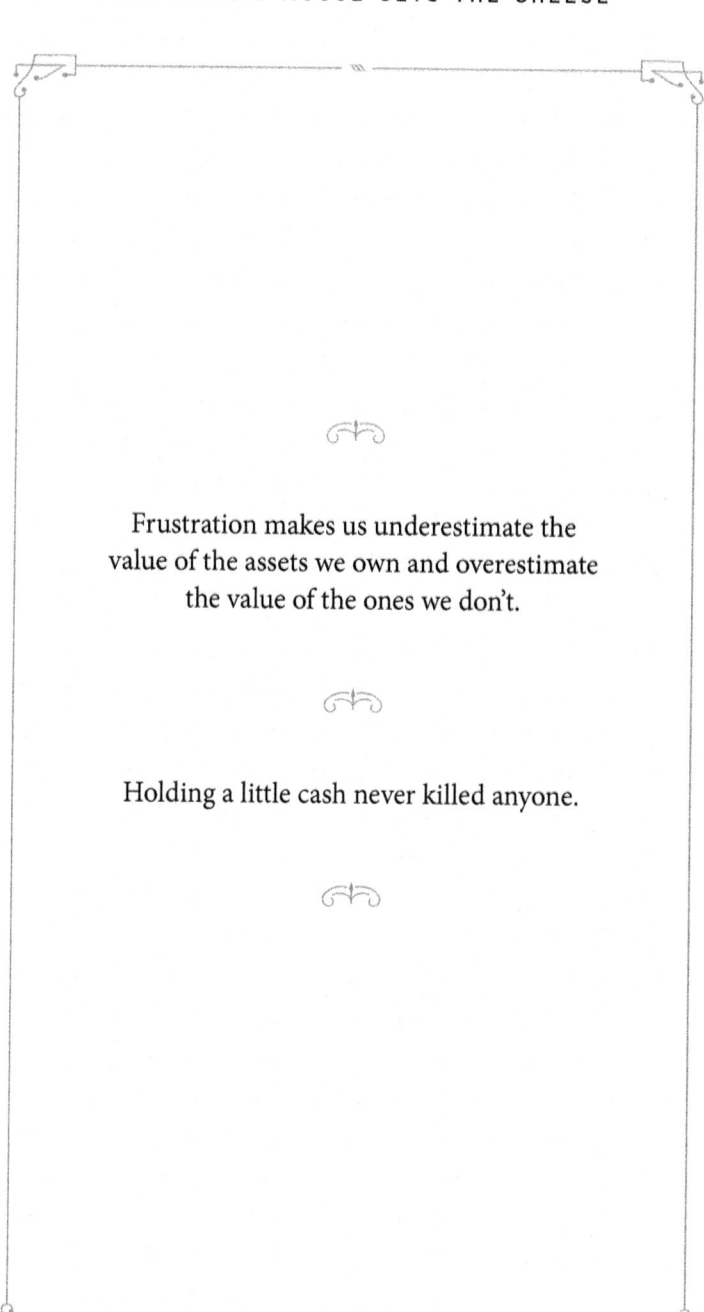

Frustration makes us underestimate the value of the assets we own and overestimate the value of the ones we don't.

Holding a little cash never killed anyone.

Ignore parenting advice from childless couples.

It is neither a requirement nor common practice for advisers to invest in the same securities they recommend to their clients. A common excuse offered by advisers is that their clients' goals and situations differ from their own, so their portfolios should also differ. That argument is most frequently heard from a salesman or asset-gatherer, however, not an investor. The most successful professional investors typically invest substantial portions of their net worth in the funds and securities they manage.

Cash flow, valuation, profitability, competitive situation, capital structure—these factors are constant in determining an investment's attractiveness. Different people have different liquidity needs, of course, but an attractive stock investment is an attractive stock investment, regardless of who owns the shares.

The caveat against taking advice from advisers or investors who don't eat their own cooking is especially critical when their recommendation is a structured product. If someone recommends that you purchase a non-traded REIT, annuity, limited partnership or unit investment trust, ask how much of the adviser's own wealth he is investing. His answer should give you a good indication of his confidence in the investment.

Always understand the other guy's motivations.

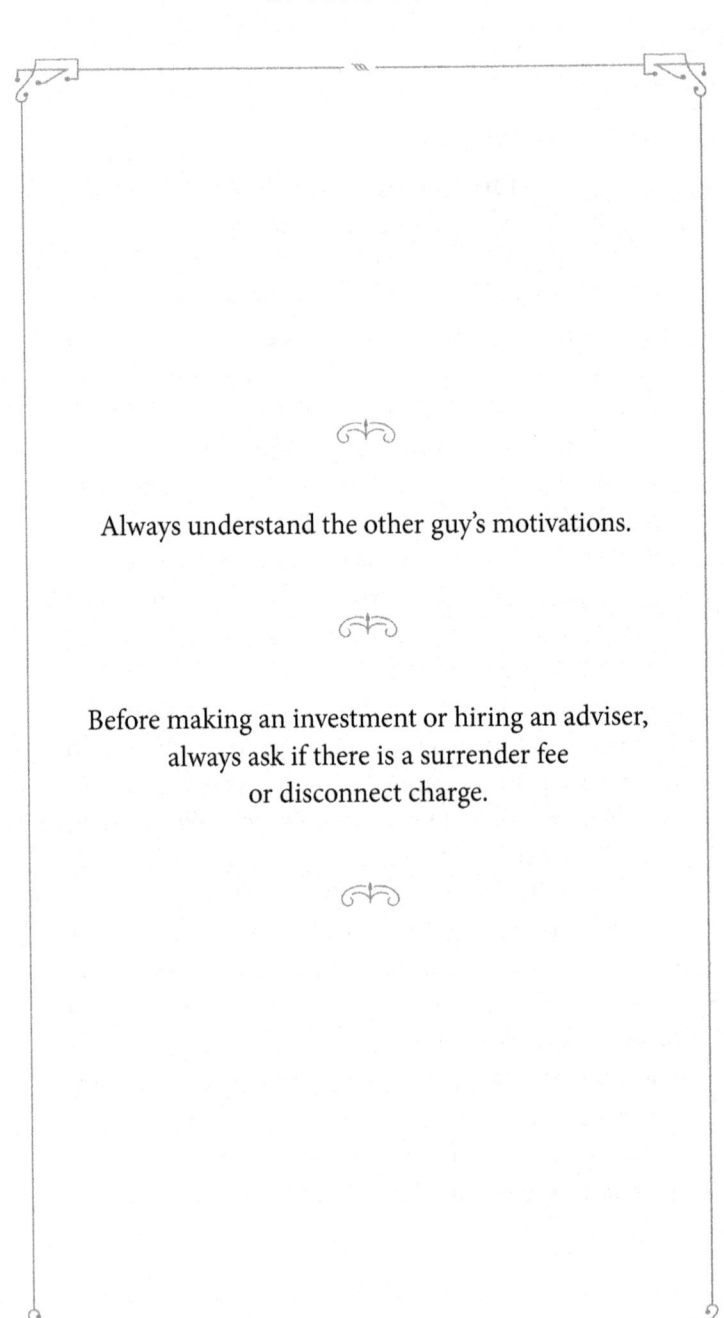

Before making an investment or hiring an adviser, always ask if there is a surrender fee or disconnect charge.

It is common sense—not rude—to ask
a prospective investment adviser if he or his firm
has ever been sued.

More client-adviser conflicts exist in
various parts of the financial industry than
most investors will ever realize.

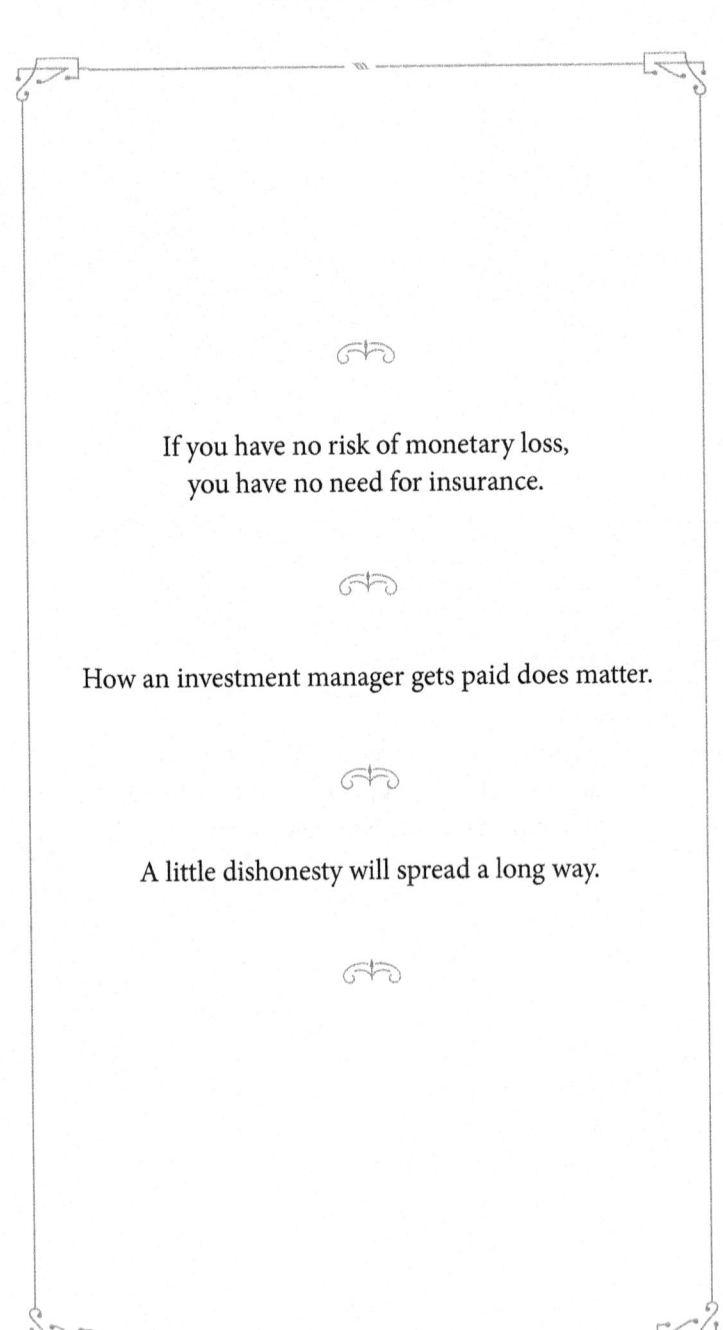

If you have no risk of monetary loss,
you have no need for insurance.

How an investment manager gets paid does matter.

A little dishonesty will spread a long way.

THE SECOND MOUSE GETS THE CHEESE

"I DON'T CARE IF HE'S STUPID. HE CAN READ AND HAS GREAT HAIR."

Experts on television are usually chosen for their communication skills and availability.

"Structured investment products" are created for the well-being of the promoters and salesmen, not investors.

When someone recommends an investment to you, ask how much of his money is in it.

When someone recommends that you buy an annuity in your IRA, end the meeting.

Life insurance on children is a wonderful benefit—
for the insurance salesman.

Never trust the promoters of a small oil
or gas exploration company.

Stockbrokers now call themselves "wealth advisers."
Apparently, too many of them took the
title "broker" literally.

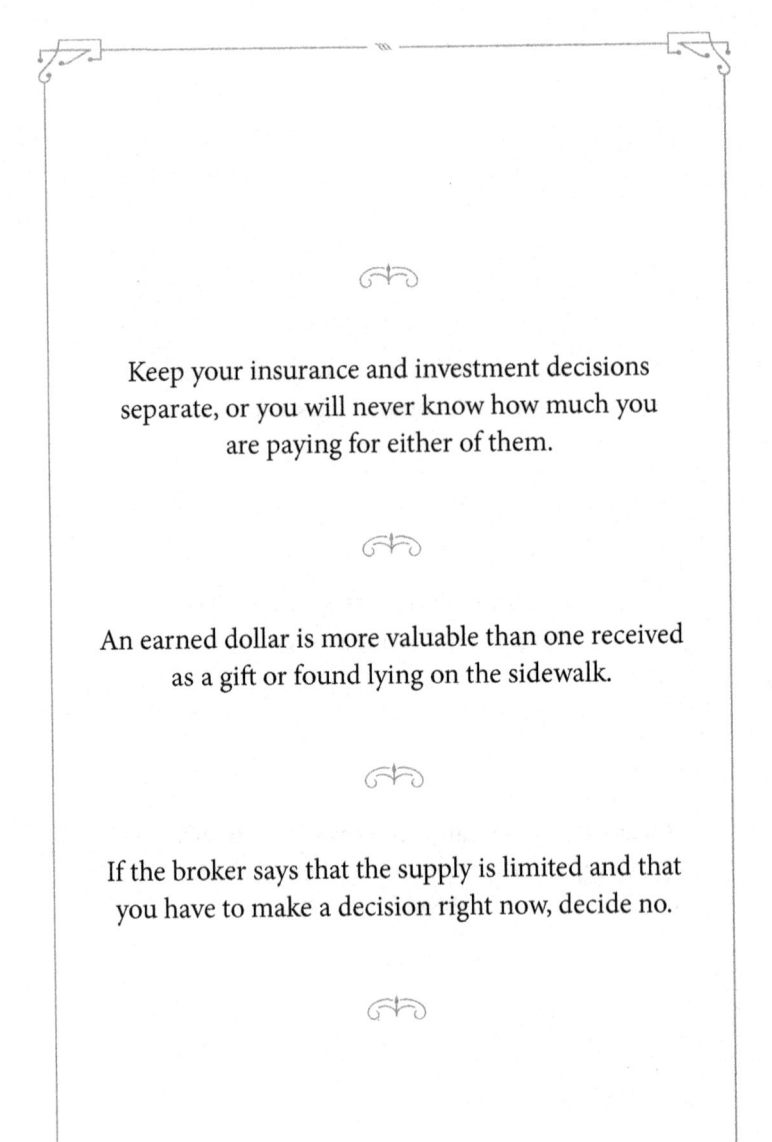

Keep your insurance and investment decisions separate, or you will never know how much you are paying for either of them.

An earned dollar is more valuable than one received as a gift or found lying on the sidewalk.

If the broker says that the supply is limited and that you have to make a decision right now, decide no.

Falling stock prices help long-term investors,
and hurt stock promoters.

John Gotti wore $2,000 Italian suits. Don't be swayed
by an investment adviser's attire.

Beware the investment adviser whose
car-to-house cost ratio exceeds 10%.

A local financial planner or guy at your church
will not figure out how to successfully time
the stock market.

Some people would rather be wrong than different.

The most frequent cause of death among zebras in the wild isn't being killed by larger, vicious predators. It is starvation. Zebras live in herds, which is very effective for defending against lion and tiger attacks, but there is little good grass available to eat in the middle of the herd.

Investment managers act a lot like zebras.

There is an uncanny similarity among the specific investments owned by a huge percentage of the professional investors. If a manager's returns deviate too far from those of his competitors, clients will move money to the better-performing managers. Slight deviations, however, don't result in investor or client exodus. As a result, the managers most concerned about losing their jobs or assets under management are more likely to have portfolios that own massive collections of popular stocks, regardless of their valuations or absolute investment attractiveness. These managers don't mind losing money or knowingly overpaying for stocks, as long as everyone else is losing money in the same overpriced stocks. There is comfort in remaining with the herd. This often results in managers owning huge collections of popular stocks, effectively creating a closet index portfolio, while charging fees for "active" management.

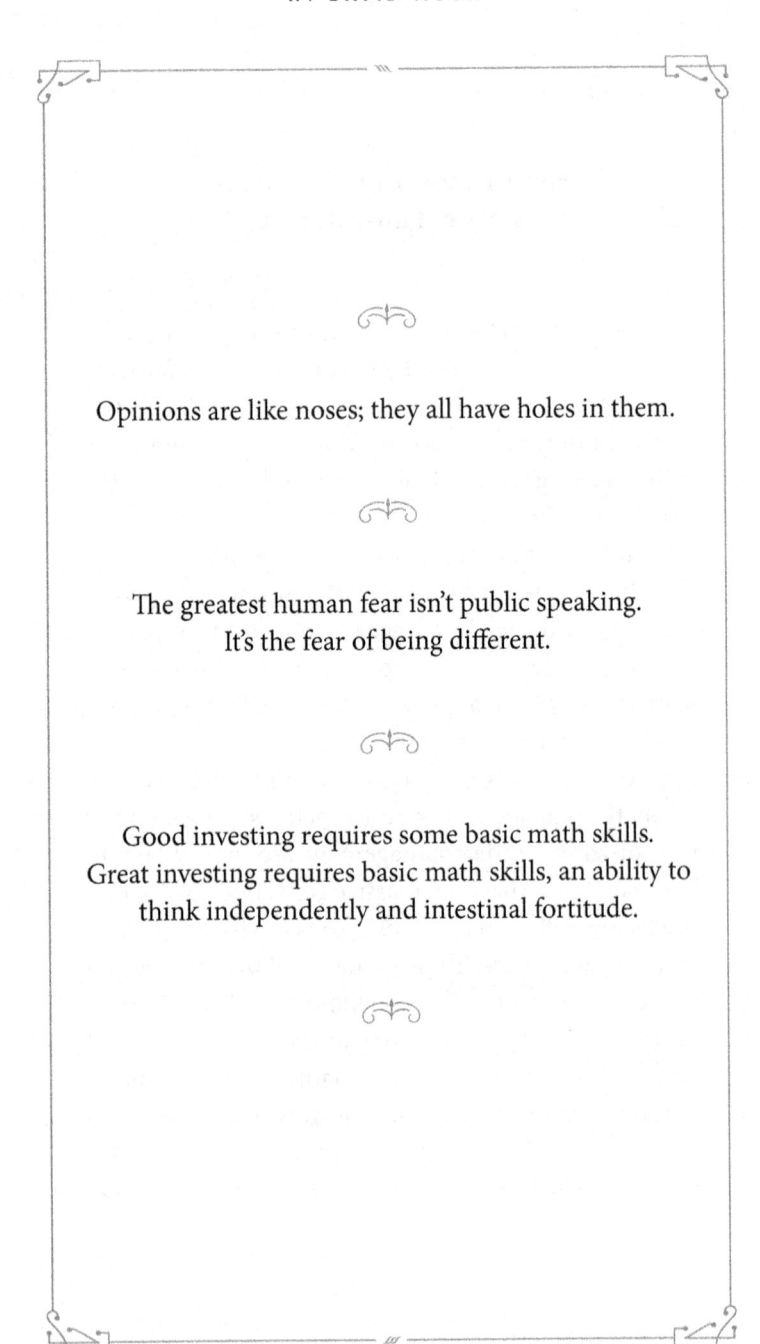

Opinions are like noses; they all have holes in them.

The greatest human fear isn't public speaking.
It's the fear of being different.

Good investing requires some basic math skills.
Great investing requires basic math skills, an ability to
think independently and intestinal fortitude.

Never underestimate the masses' insistence on remaining irrational.

Most investors, like automobile drivers, think they are better than average.

Like great comedians, great investors look at the same information as everyone else—and see it just a bit differently.

Investors need a healthy dose of both optimism and skepticism. A lack of either can be disastrous.

Any time that you spend thinking about the money you've lost in the market is time you could be thinking about the money you still have invested in the market.

It is human nature to believe what you are told and then look for confirming evidence. Great investors are skeptics who look for evidence that they are wrong.

Don't base your 401(k) investments on your co-worker's decisions. He probably just copied someone else.

Bragging about one's investment or romantic exploits reveals an embarrassing lack of confidence.

When someone gives you a stock tip, is it to help you, make himself look good or convince you to do something that might benefit him?

Never buy an investment simply (or even mostly) because you heard that some rich guys were investing in it.

Never confuse someone's ability to communicate with his ability to think.

CNBC broadcasts 24 hours a day. Everyone on earth will eventually appear on the network.

The amount of newsprint or bandwidth used to report a story is not a measure of its significance.

Seek information that challenges your conclusions, not affirms them.

An annual report is neither true fact nor true fiction. It is more like a docudrama, where the bad guys can be disguised by the accountants.

A manager's past performance is no guarantee of future results, but it's as good a guide as any.

Someone has to win coin flipping contests.

Imagine there are 1,000 people split into 500 pairs, engaged in a coin flipping contest. After the first round, 500 winners would advance into round 2, continuing the process until a single person remained. The person would have correctly "predicted" the outcome 11 consecutive times and could claim to be in the top one-tenth of all coin flip predictors, even though his flipping tournament victory was simply a string of 50/50 chance outcomes.

We often mistake luck and randomness for skill.

In the late 1990s, a number of investors filled their portfolios with stocks of unprofitable companies, simply based on those companies' connection to the Internet. Most of the businesses had no profits; some didn't have revenues. These new experts explained that old valuation metrics were no longer relevant. They were praised for their investment results and heralded (by themselves and others) as visionary geniuses. That is until the Internet bubble burst, exposing these supposed prescient prodigies as winners in a coin flipping contest.

The inherent randomness of the stock market means that some unskilled investors are bound to produce great short-term performance records. Sometimes people get lucky. Be careful not to confuse that with talent.

Any creative fifth grader can formulate an investment strategy that worked great in the past.

If you're going to gamble, do it in Las Vegas, not on Wall Street. At least in Vegas you get watered-down drinks and Wayne Newton.

Your largest possible loss is the same on a $3 stock as it is on a $30 stock: 100%.

If you don't always play the odds, don't ever play them.

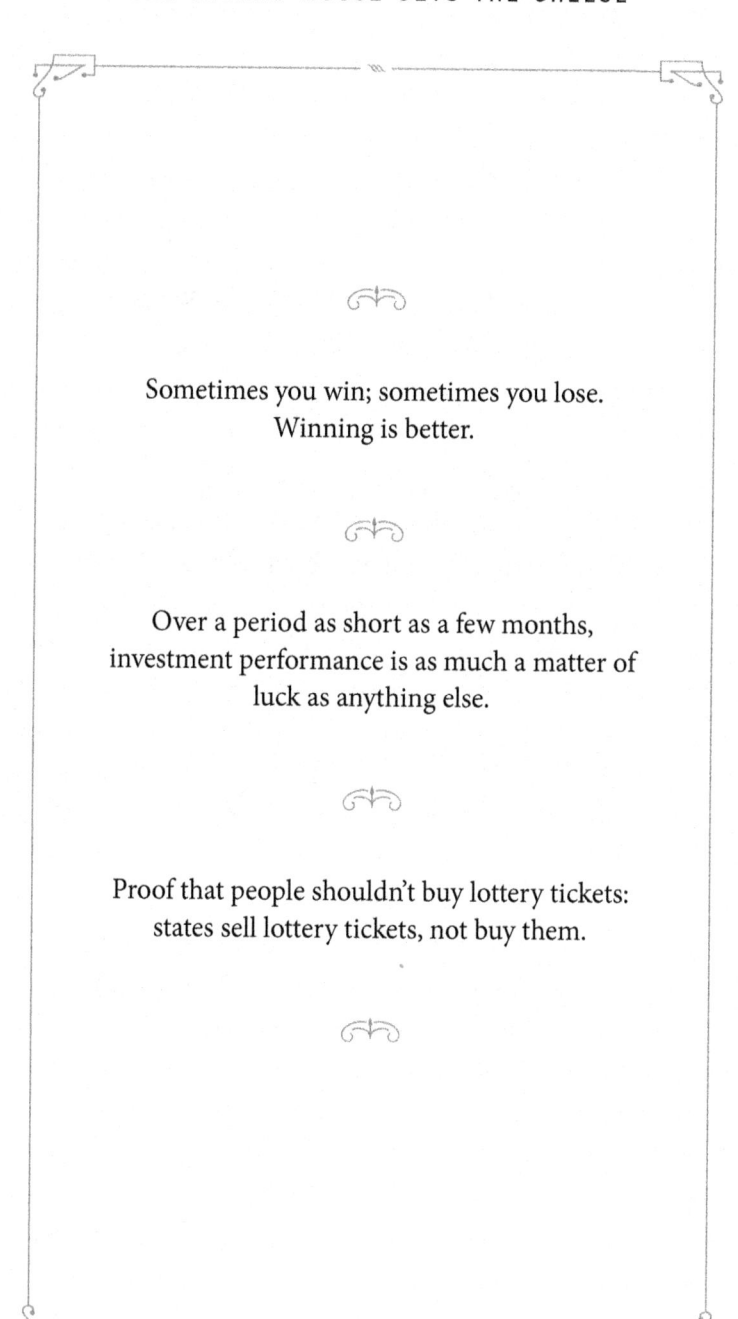

Sometimes you win; sometimes you lose.
Winning is better.

Over a period as short as a few months, investment performance is as much a matter of luck as anything else.

Proof that people shouldn't buy lottery tickets: states sell lottery tickets, not buy them.

Getting lucky can create an undeserved confidence.

Banks are in the asset gathering,
deposit and loan business. They are generally
terrible mutual fund managers.

If you don't respect your crazy brother's opinion about politics, why listen to his investment tips?

Spend your time studying investments, not trying to predict the economy or the market.

THE SECOND MOUSE GETS THE CHEESE

[Cartoon: Two economists stranded on a small island with a palm tree. One says in a thought bubble: "LET'S JUST ASSUME WE HAVE AN OUTLET TO RECHARGE OUR SMARTPHONES, SO WE CAN CALL FOR A BOAT." Caption: ECONOMISTS STRANDED ON AN ISLAND]

Academicians' theories often start with the assumption that there are no taxes or transaction costs. This alone is enough to dismiss them.

Hire an accountant whose own tax return is at least as complicated as yours.

Presidents, like quarterbacks, tend to get way too much credit when things go well and too much blame when they don't.

When something is in writing, it seems so much more authoritative, even though the act of writing creates no additional validity.

If you need proof that most people think
with their heart and not their head, look at all the
money wasted on lotteries.

Pass on any company that generated
more cash selling its stock than its products in
four of the past five years.

Directors who approve stock splits either are bored
or believe their shareholders are gullible.

Someone will always have more money and bigger biceps than you.

The writer of the ancient text in the book of Deuteronomy warns against coveting thy neighbor's stuff, including his house, wife or servants. He might also have included investment returns or a 401(k).

As a discrete construct, money has no value. A net worth above a certain number may make us feel safe and provide options in life, but if a person's goal is to have the largest net worth, he is doomed to failure. This year's most wealthy individual is likely to be dethroned next year.

Jealousy motivates people to act irrationally, in both matters of the heart and the pocketbook. It obviously causes some people to buy cars, boats and houses they can't afford, but it also influences some investment decisions. Hearing a co-worker brag about having purchased Google at its IPO can create a disquieting resentfulness, inspiring even a normally rational person to take irrational risks. Measure your investment success against your goals, not the results or boasts of others.

A person can be rich in many ways. There is nothing wrong with money being one of them.

No one brags about his losers.

The difference between bankruptcy and financial independence can be as little as 15% of your monthly expenses.

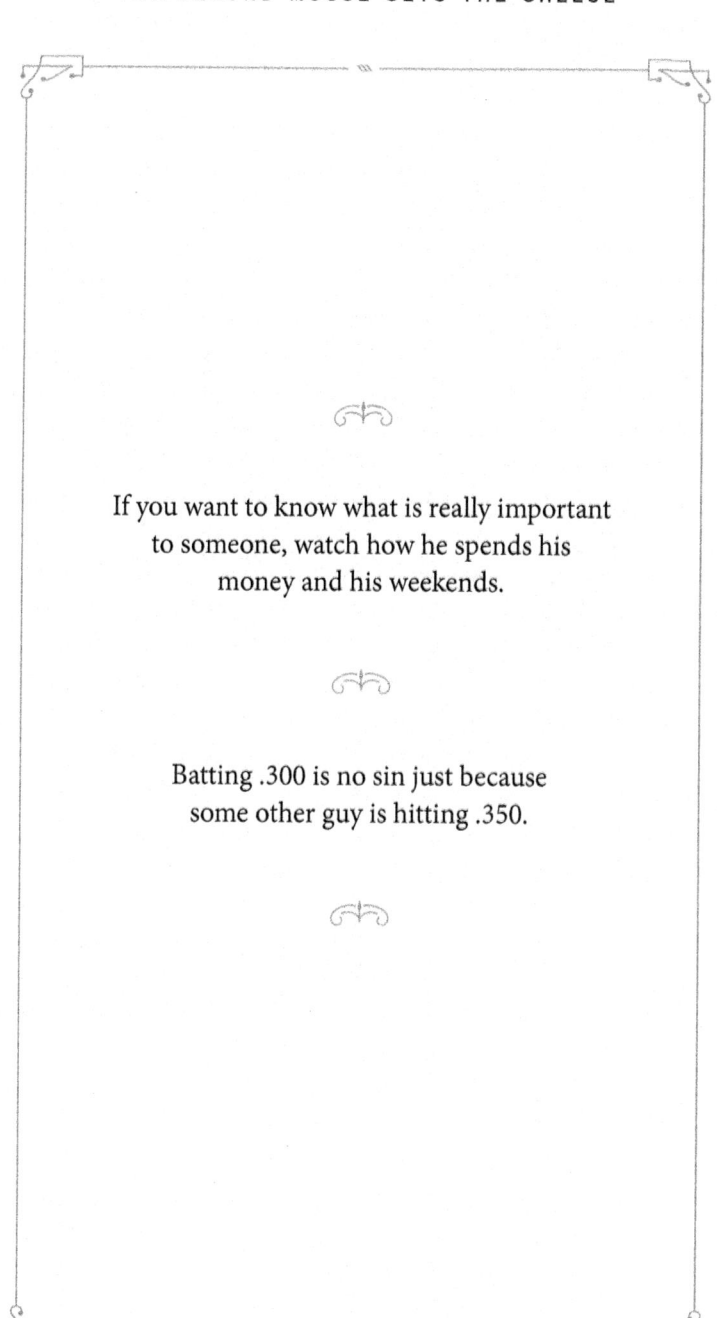

If you want to know what is really important to someone, watch how he spends his money and his weekends.

Batting .300 is no sin just because some other guy is hitting .350.

A house is not an investment. Neither are kids, but that doesn't stop us from having them.

The easiest time in life to learn to save money is when you are just a step or two above broke.

How to become a rich old person: don't lose money often, don't get divorced and don't die.

A million people claim to have seen Hank Aaron hit his 715th home run. Even more claim to have bought Google at $85 per share. Most of both groups are lying.

Real wealth is usually accumulated like excess weight: slowly, over decades.

At age 15, the gift of a lawnmower is more beneficial than the gift of cash.

Without good health and a good friend, money is worthless.

Money doesn't change people. It exposes them.

When interviewing a prospective investment adviser, ask about the investments in his portfolio.

Wealth without purpose is not only empty;
it's not much fun.

It's too late to teach a child to be responsible
with money when he is 23.

Grief and greed are kindred spirits:
a longing for something we don't have.

There's usually an inverse relationship between
the validity of someone's argument and
how loudly he presents it.

Risk-adjusted returns are for people who don't understand risk.

The term "risk-adjusted return" aims to gauge if an investor's return is suitable, given the level of risk the investor assumed. In theory, this concept makes sense and should be useful. Assume the S&P 500 increases 10% in a year. Any investor could have produced a 20% return by leveraging his account 2-to-1 with borrowed money and simply buying the S&P 500. The apparently stellar investment results would be the result of increased risk, not skillful investment analysis.

The problem with trying to measure risk-adjusted returns is that there is no precise way to measure risk. Consultants love to define risk as volatility, but that definition is as logically flawed as it is impractical. Risk is often easy to identify—such as investing with borrowed funds—but it is very difficult to quantify.

"Risk-adjusted returns" do give advisers and consultants either a convenient excuse for their disappointing results or a rationale for the exceptional results of someone else. Warren Buffett produced his outstanding track record while taking less risk than the overall market—a concept that doesn't make sense to people who don't understand risk.

Beware of false precision.

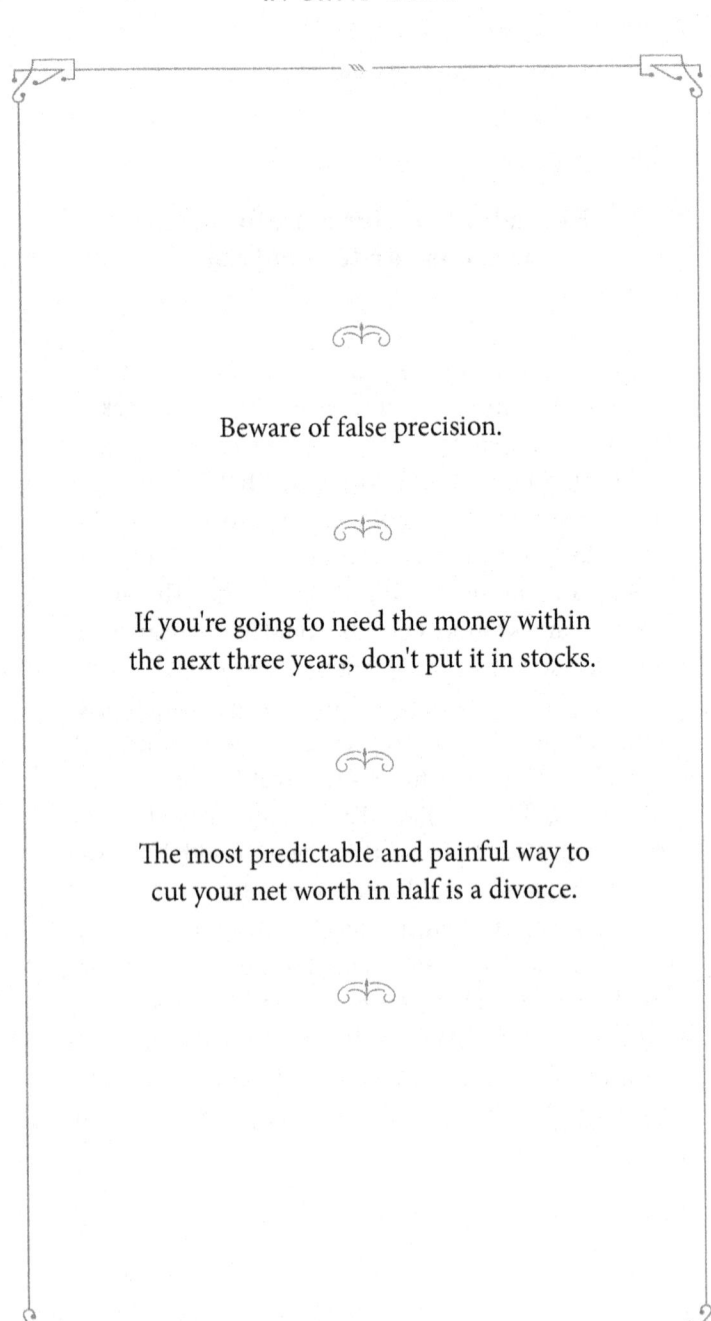

If you're going to need the money within the next three years, don't put it in stocks.

The most predictable and painful way to cut your net worth in half is a divorce.

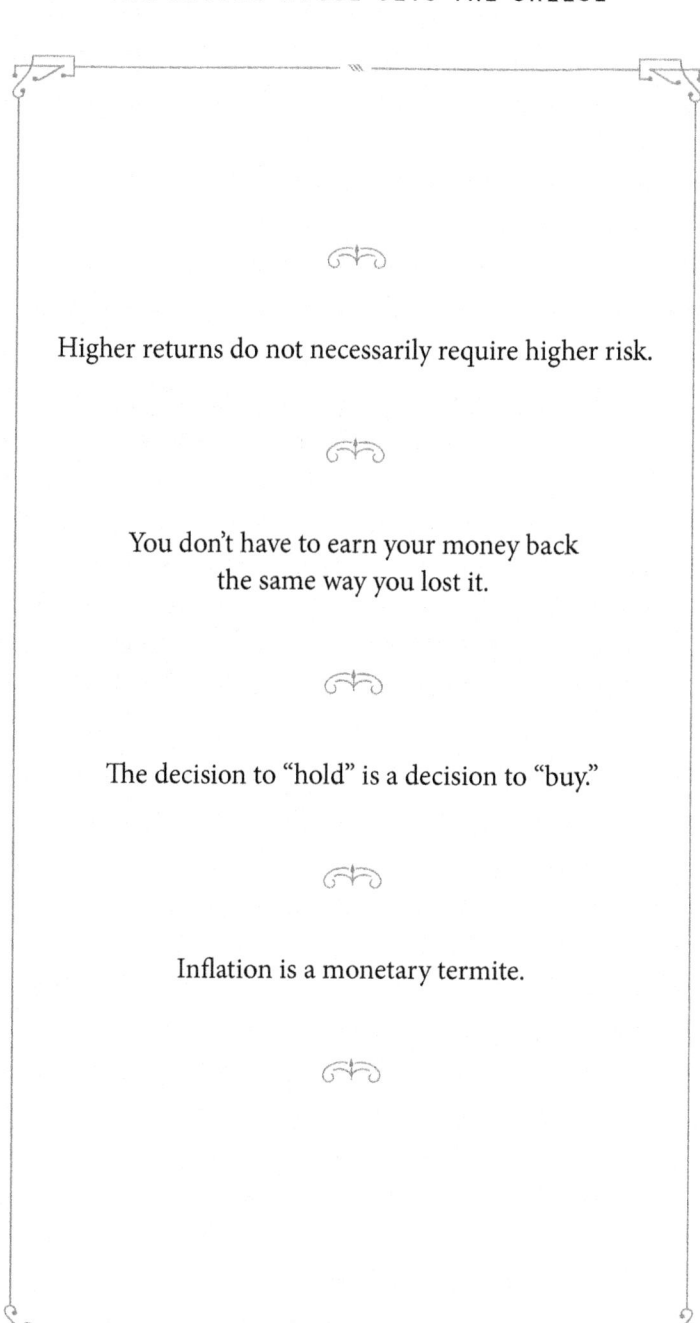

Higher returns do not necessarily require higher risk.

You don't have to earn your money back
the same way you lost it.

The decision to "hold" is a decision to "buy."

Inflation is a monetary termite.

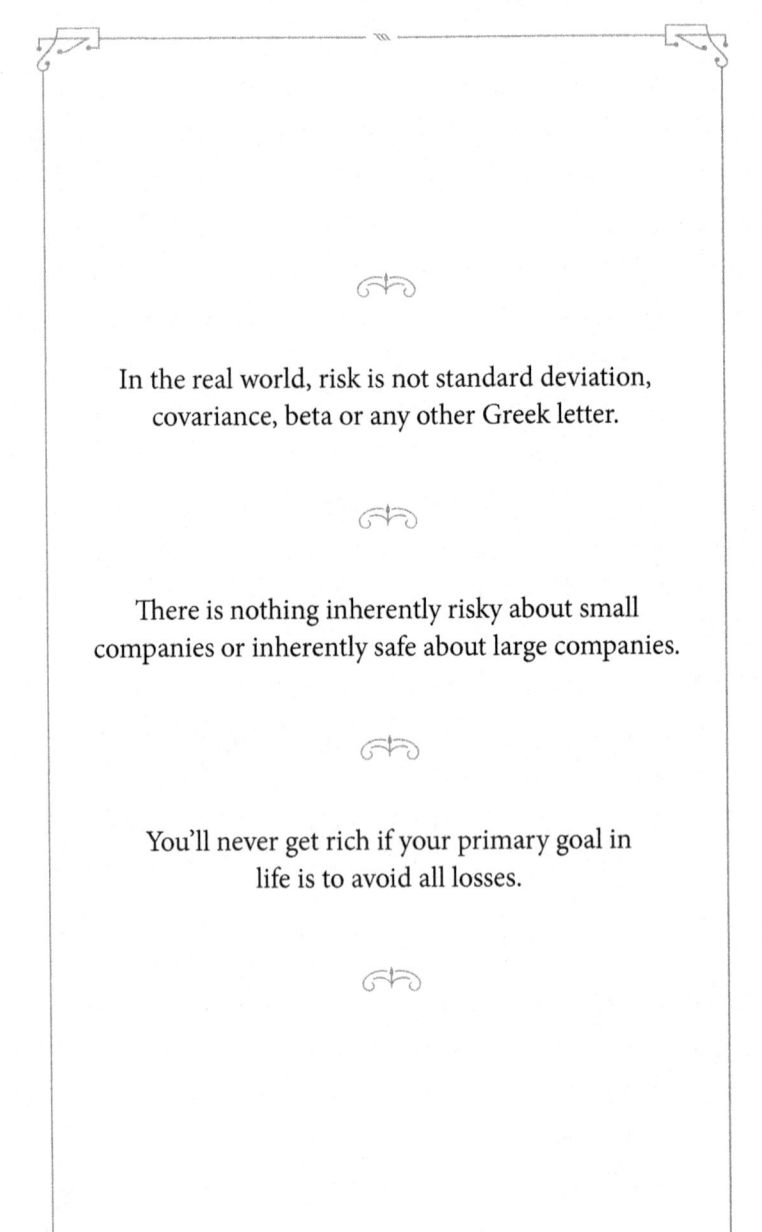

In the real world, risk is not standard deviation, covariance, beta or any other Greek letter.

There is nothing inherently risky about small companies or inherently safe about large companies.

You'll never get rich if your primary goal in life is to avoid all losses.

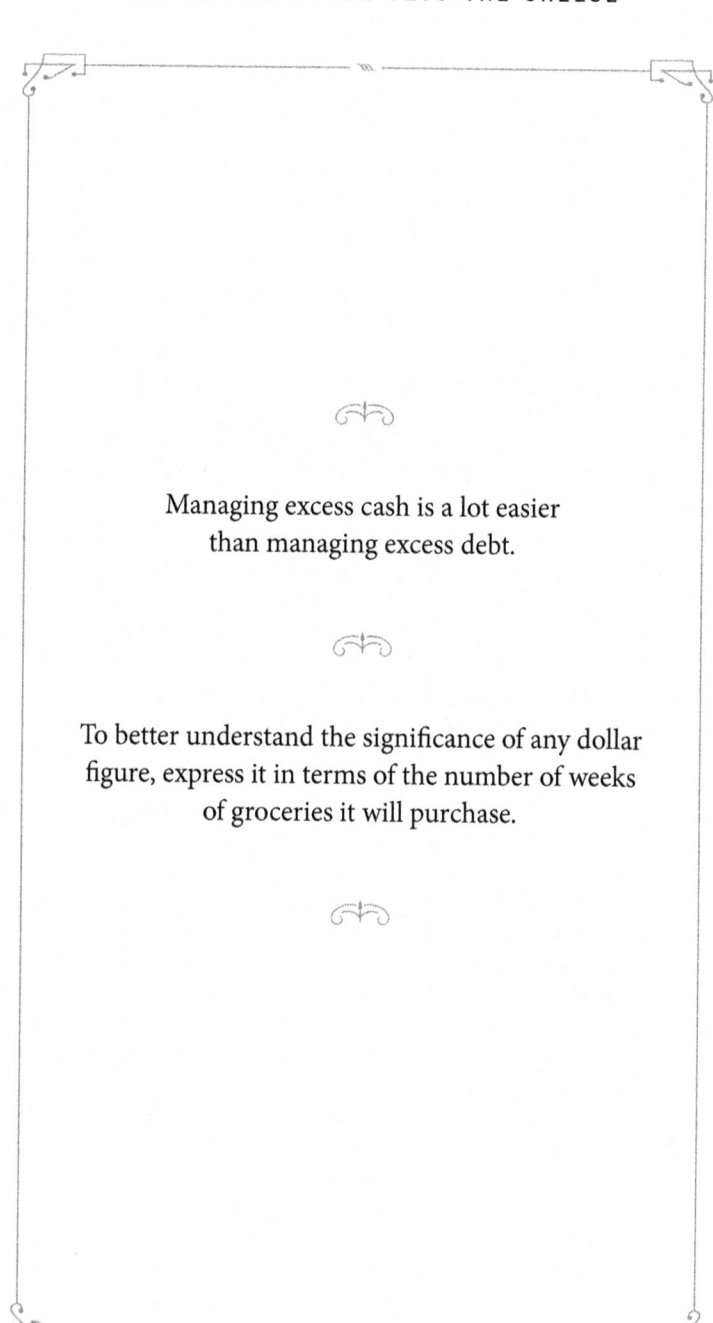

Managing excess cash is a lot easier
than managing excess debt.

To better understand the significance of any dollar figure, express it in terms of the number of weeks of groceries it will purchase.

Investment risk is determined by the business dynamics and the financial characteristics of a company along with the price you pay for the company's stock.

The risk-free rate of return only exists in college lectures and textbooks.

Risk cannot be calculated to two decimal places.

THE SECOND MOUSE GETS THE CHEESE

"JUST IGNORE THAT. IT'S STANDARD LEGAL BOILERPLATE."

When the prospectus for an investment states, "These securities involve a high degree of risk," believe it.

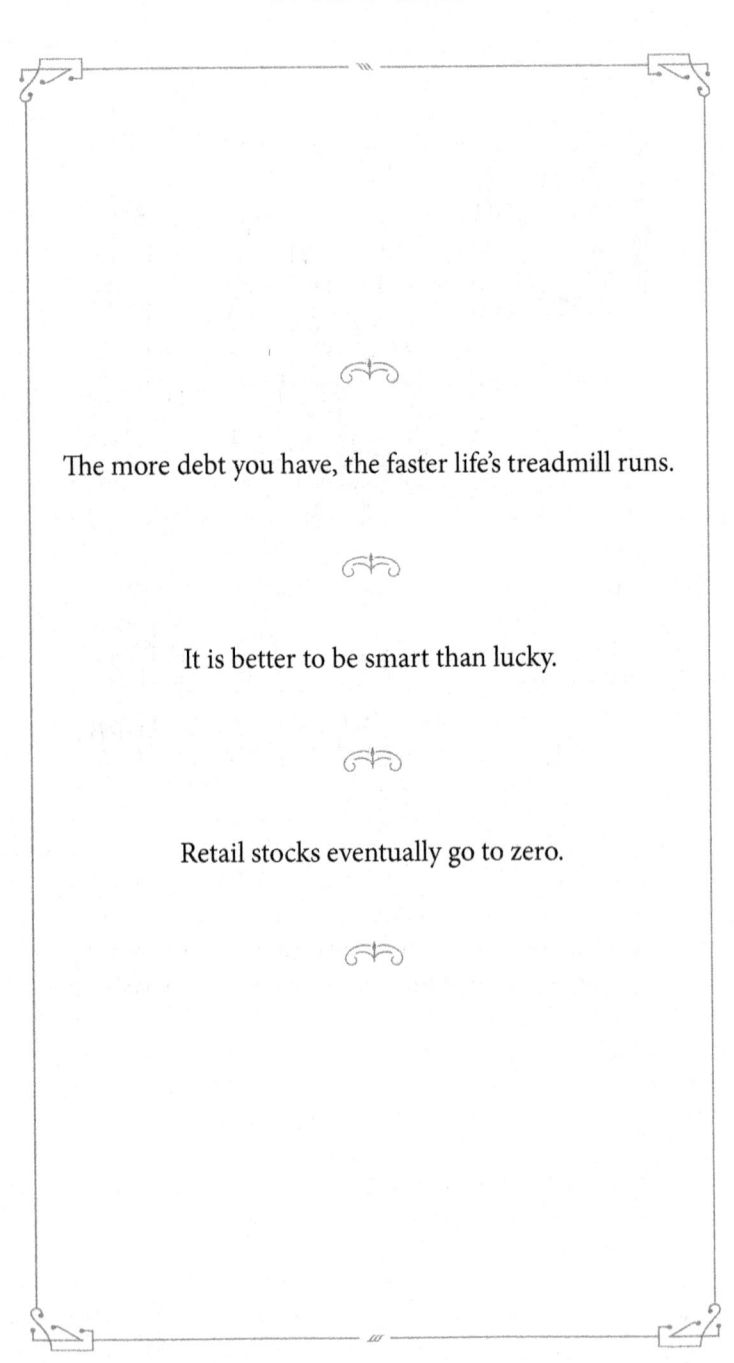

The more debt you have, the faster life's treadmill runs.

It is better to be smart than lucky.

Retail stocks eventually go to zero.

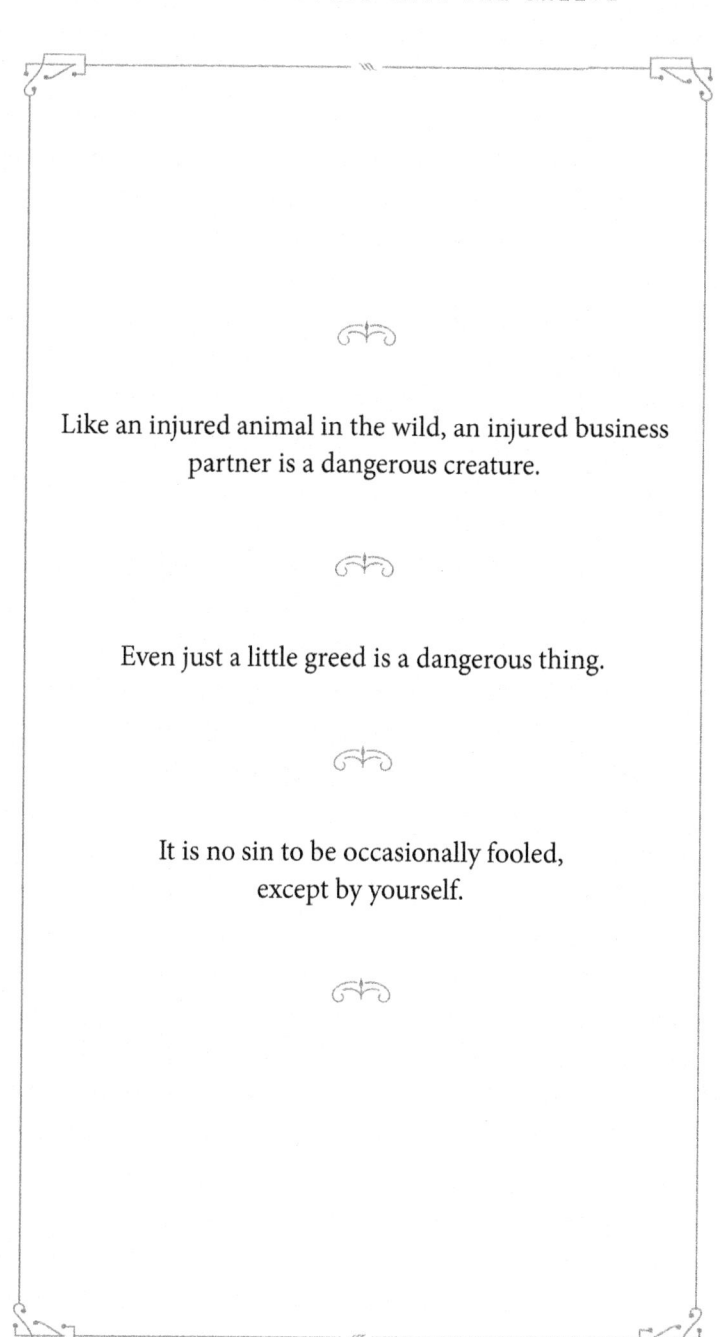

Like an injured animal in the wild, an injured business partner is a dangerous creature.

Even just a little greed is a dangerous thing.

It is no sin to be occasionally fooled, except by yourself.

Overdiversification is an inept way to overcome a lack of knowledge.

Business schools teach that the answer to every investment problem is "diversify." If you're not sure what to do, diversify. If you're just getting started, diversify. If you're nearing retirement, diversify. If you're conservative, diversify. Aggressive? Diversify. If you hate your mother, want to lose weight or quit smoking, diversify, diversify, diversify.

The "diversify more" portfolio should hold big stocks, little stocks, medium-size stocks, growth stocks, value stocks and hard-to-classify stocks. Domestic stocks, foreign stocks, multinational stocks, livestock and Woodstock. Taxable and nontaxable bonds. Real estate, both commercial and residential. Undeveloped land. Storage buildings, cattle farms and vacation property.

And don't forget investments in hard assets like gold, silver and weapons-grade plutonium.

When they don't know what to do, some people do nothing. Others do everything—a little of that, a little of this, and this, and this. Overdiversification is how some people seek to overcome a lack of knowledge, but when you diversify a portfolio to the point that you own everything, you've guaranteed mediocrity—less your costs, of course.

It is better to own a few things that you know well
than a highly diversified portfolio about which
you know little of substance.

If you own eight or more mutual funds, you have
created a very expensive index fund.

The mantra of the indexer: If you don't know
much about what you are buying,
buy a little bit of everything.

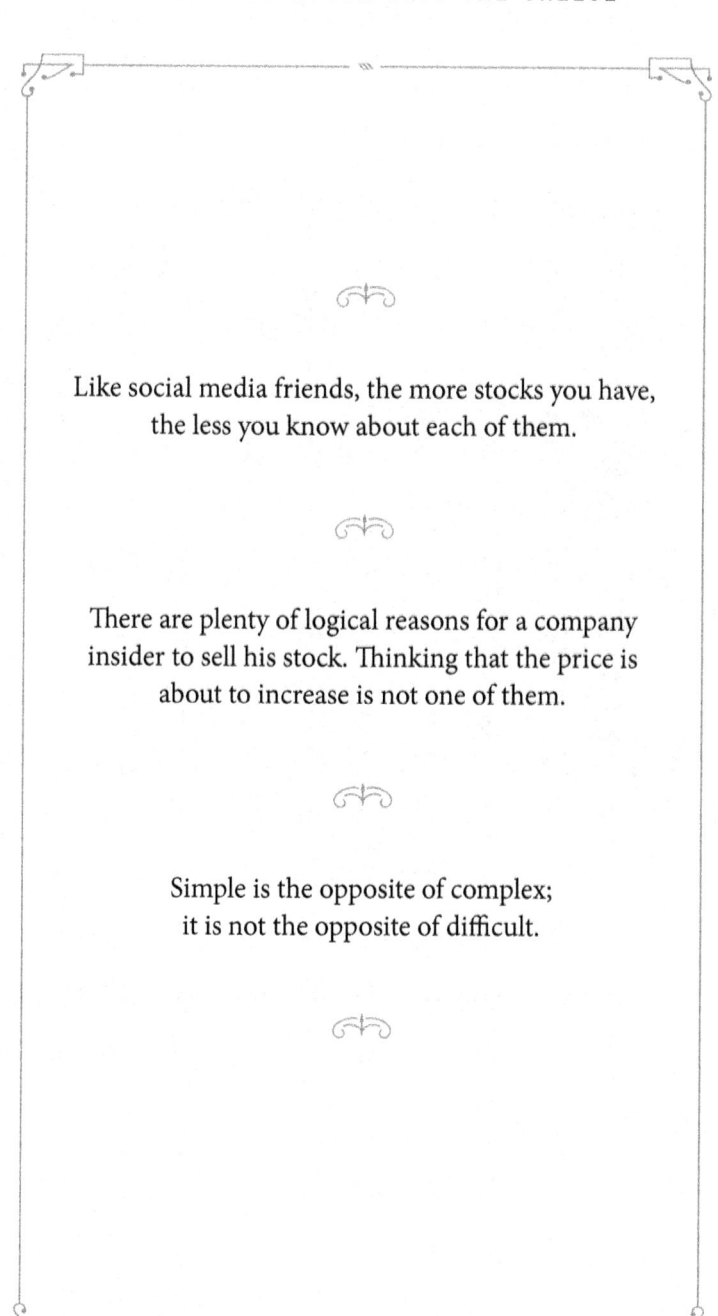

Like social media friends, the more stocks you have, the less you know about each of them.

There are plenty of logical reasons for a company insider to sell his stock. Thinking that the price is about to increase is not one of them.

Simple is the opposite of complex; it is not the opposite of difficult.

People who don't know what they're doing buy a little bit of everything and call it diversification.

There is a big difference between
"investing" and "collecting."

Chasing the one lost sheep might be a great
way to shepherd, but it is a terrible way to invest.
Pay attention to the 99 you have,
not the one you missed.

"Mutual fund," like "IRA," is a generic term and is not
a description of the risk or safety of an investment.

An investor can adequately diversify his
portfolio with 20 different stocks.

Football season doesn't cause the leaves to change colors.

It is human nature to "find" patterns where none exist or to ascribe causality among events that happen to merely coincide with each other. In 1926, George Taylor posited that in booming economic times women would wear shorter dresses in order to show off their expensive silk stockings, foretelling of higher future stock prices. As income and wealth declined, hemlines would lengthen, hiding a woman's inability to afford such luxuries, and acting as a precursor to falling stock prices. Some investors still seriously discuss this hemline theory of stock price movement.

Events often follow sequential patterns without being causally related. Snowstorms cause both increased automobile accidents and the sale of sleds, but neither sled sales nor car wrecks cause the other.

We tend to look for predictable relationships to explain the world around us, despite there being no causal relationship between many highly correlated items. This sort of reasoning is tempting because it requires little thought or energy. It is also often flawed.

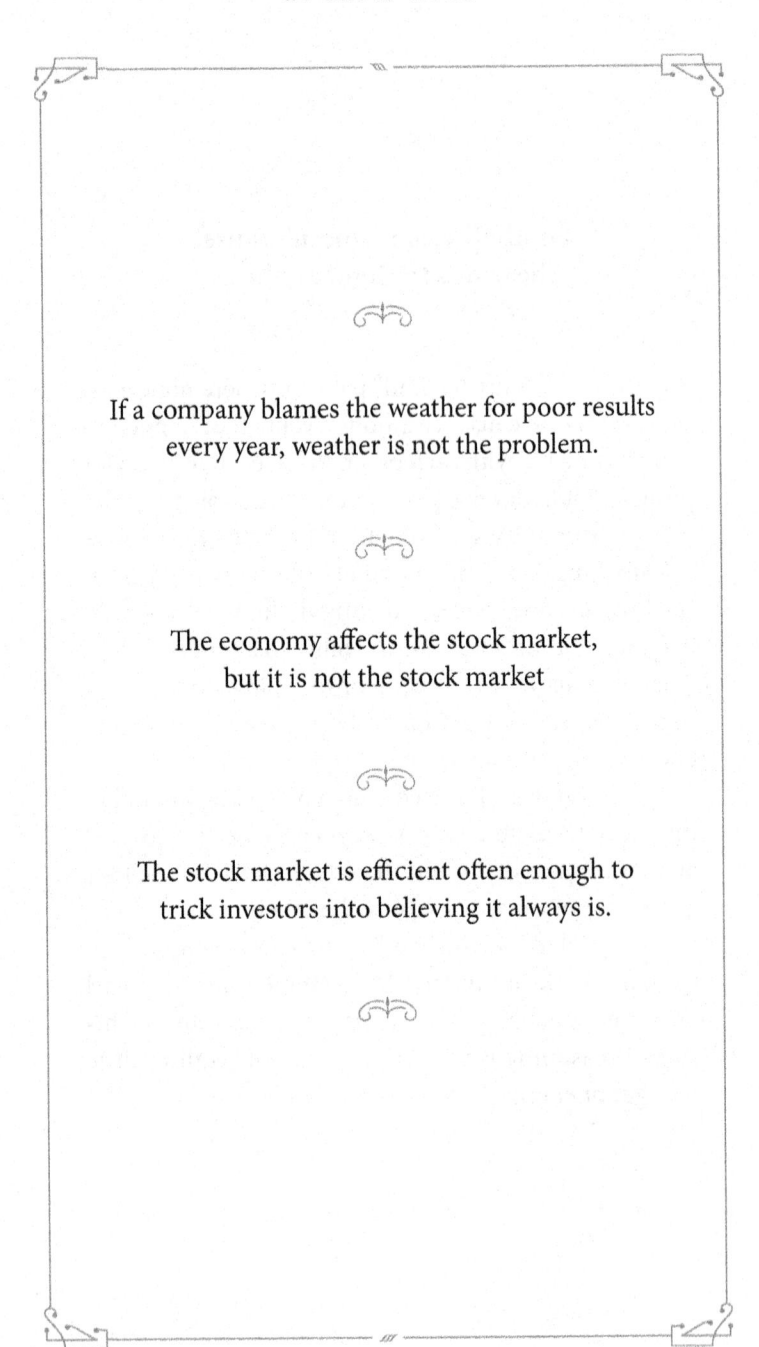

If a company blames the weather for poor results every year, weather is not the problem.

The economy affects the stock market, but it is not the stock market

The stock market is efficient often enough to trick investors into believing it always is.

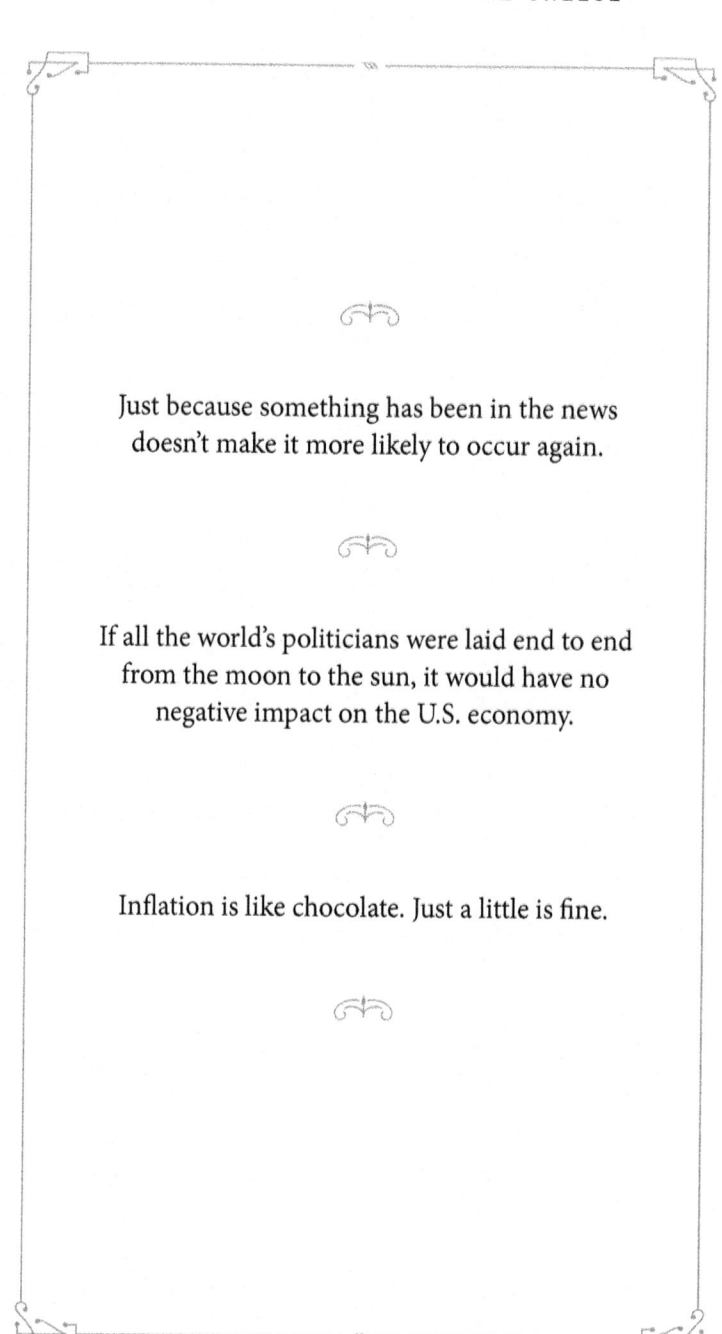

Just because something has been in the news doesn't make it more likely to occur again.

If all the world's politicians were laid end to end from the moon to the sun, it would have no negative impact on the U.S. economy.

Inflation is like chocolate. Just a little is fine.

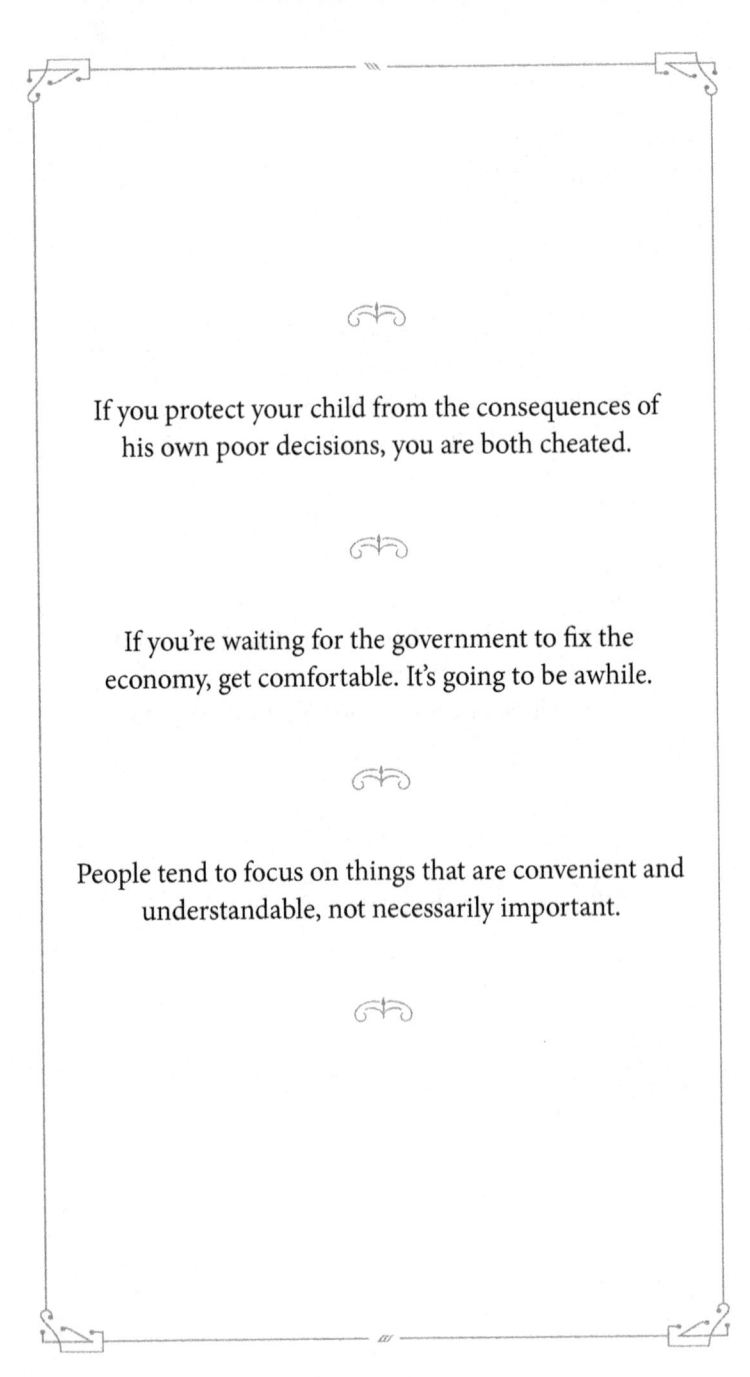

If you protect your child from the consequences of his own poor decisions, you are both cheated.

If you're waiting for the government to fix the economy, get comfortable. It's going to be awhile.

People tend to focus on things that are convenient and understandable, not necessarily important.

THE SECOND MOUSE GETS THE CHEESE

"I'M SURE GLAD INFLATION IS ONLY 2%."

If you want to know the inflation rate, look at your checkbook records over the past three years, not reports from the Bureau of Labor Statistics.

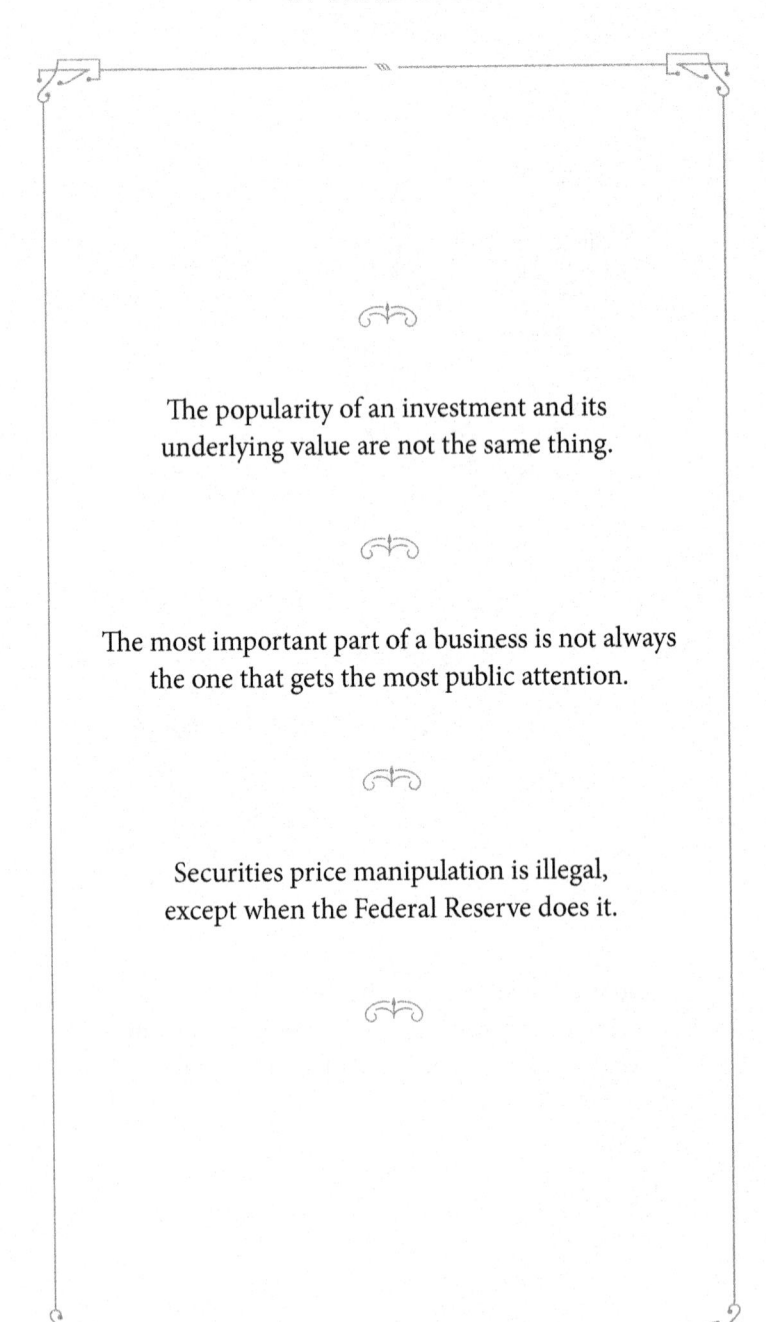

The popularity of an investment and its underlying value are not the same thing.

The most important part of a business is not always the one that gets the most public attention.

Securities price manipulation is illegal, except when the Federal Reserve does it.

If CNBC reported it this morning, it's probably already factored into the price of a stock.

War and rumors of war are terrible reasons to sell stocks.

We tend to overestimate the likelihood of rare, but well publicized, possible events that might affect the economy. It is the unpublicized event that is the greatest risk.

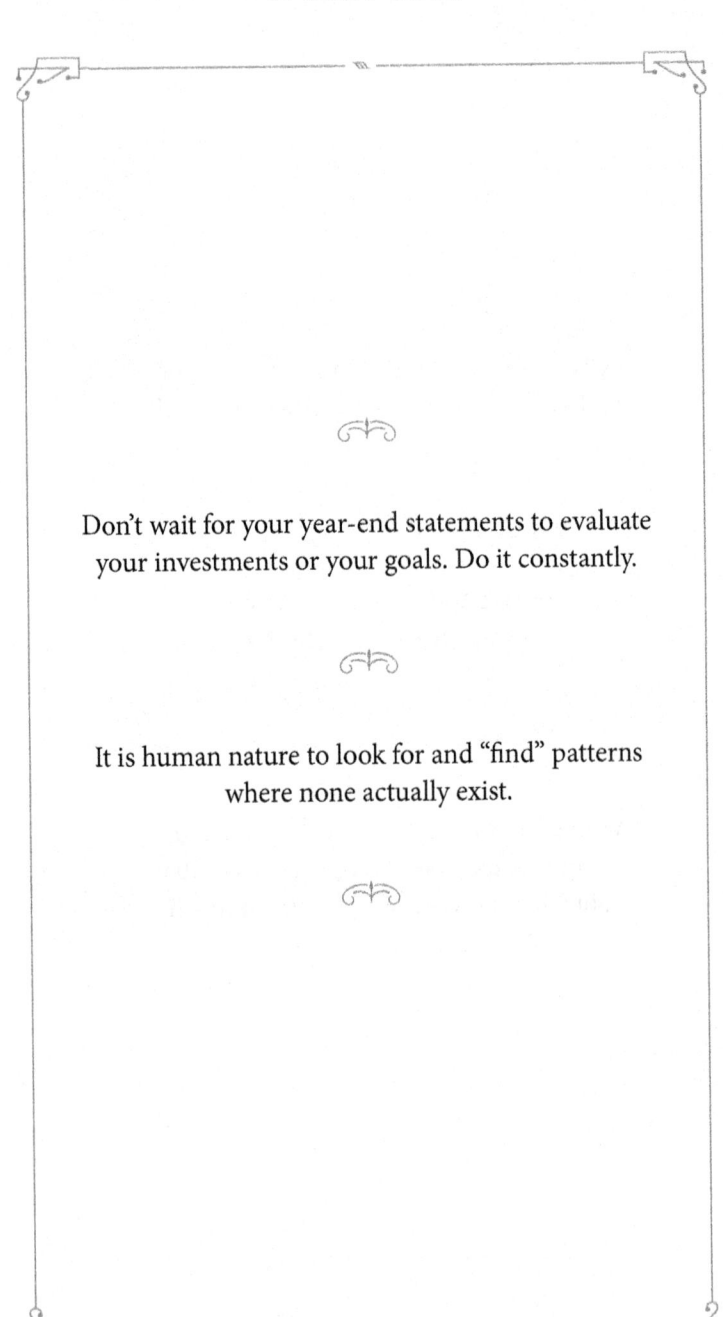

Don't wait for your year-end statements to evaluate your investments or your goals. Do it constantly.

It is human nature to look for and "find" patterns where none actually exist.

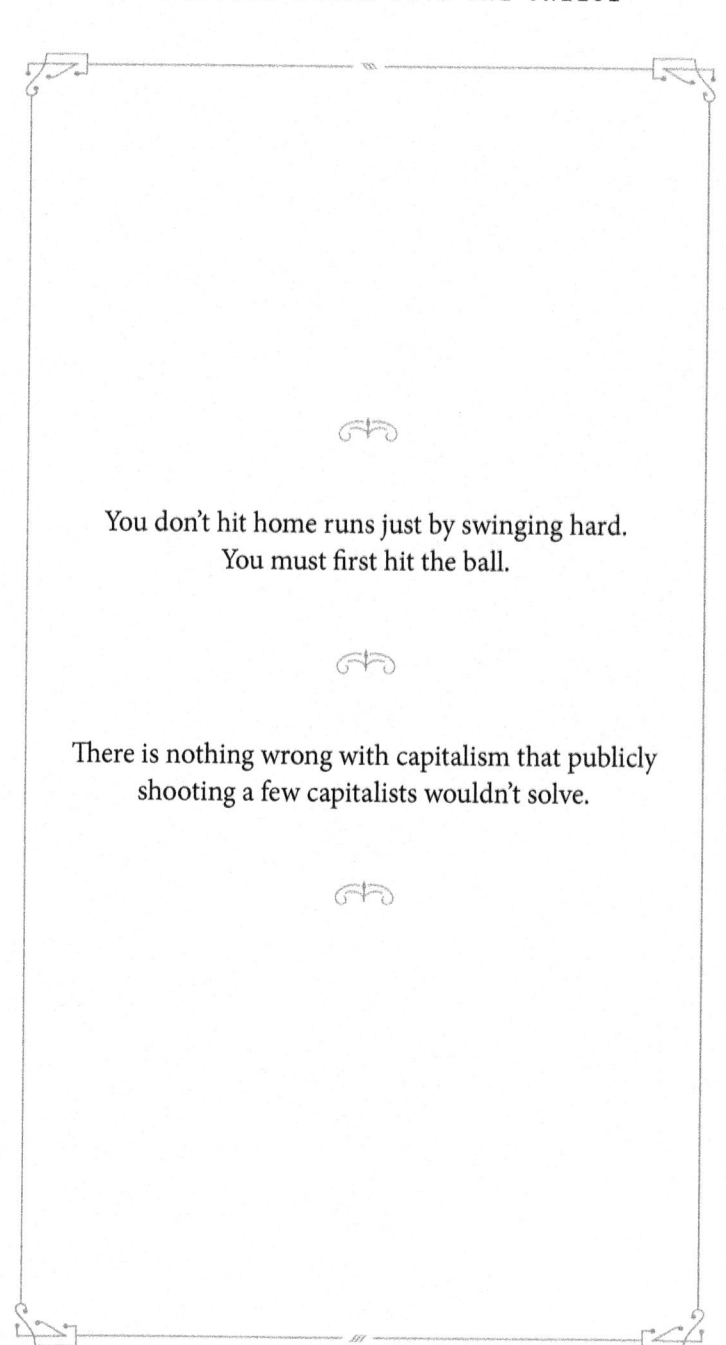

You don't hit home runs just by swinging hard.
You must first hit the ball.

There is nothing wrong with capitalism that publicly
shooting a few capitalists wouldn't solve.

Isaac Newton was not an investment analyst.

No prospective home buyer ever waited for a seller to raise his price before making an offer; yet stock investors regularly do so, buying shares simply because of recent price increases. An entire branch of finance, technical analysis, is built around the false notion that, like physical masses drawn together by gravity, a stock price tends to continue moving in its most recent direction until interrupted by an outside force.

Technical analysis is the antithesis of fundamental analysis. It presumes that the future price of a stock is a function of its past price, irrespective of the underlying business, its profitability, competitive situation or capital structure. It is akin to using historical results from flipping a coin to predict the outcome of the next toss. The results of the previous 100 tosses might produce long win streaks for heads, but the odds of getting heads on the next toss are 50%. The coin has no memory and is uninfluenced by inertia.

Technical analysis is seductive because it incorporates mystery, simplicity and precision. Of course, so do Ouija boards and Tarot cards.

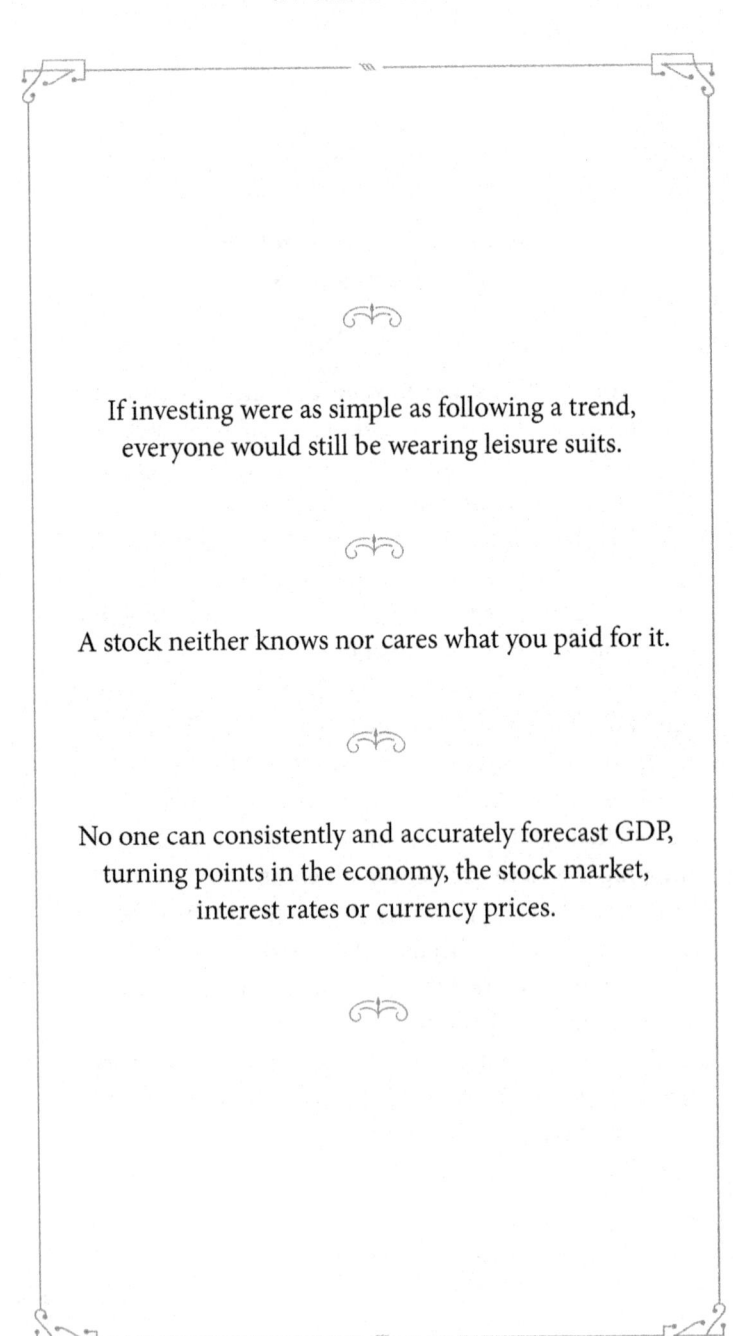

If investing were as simple as following a trend, everyone would still be wearing leisure suits.

A stock neither knows nor cares what you paid for it.

No one can consistently and accurately forecast GDP, turning points in the economy, the stock market, interest rates or currency prices.

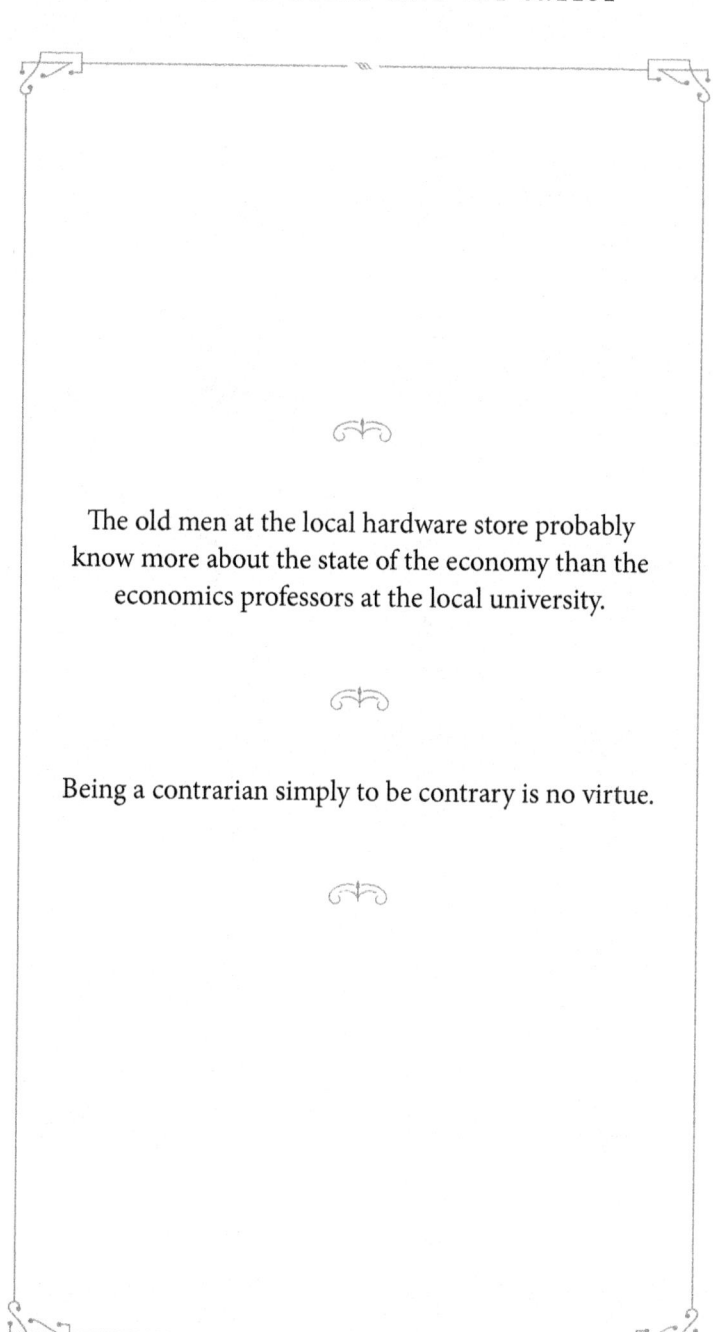

The old men at the local hardware store probably know more about the state of the economy than the economics professors at the local university.

Being a contrarian simply to be contrary is no virtue.

"TODAY DATA CLOUDS OVER SILICON VALLEY, CALIFORNIA, TAX INCREASES IN ILLINOIS, A TWEET STORM IN WASHINGTON, D.C..."

Predicting the weather is easier than predicting Congressional action.

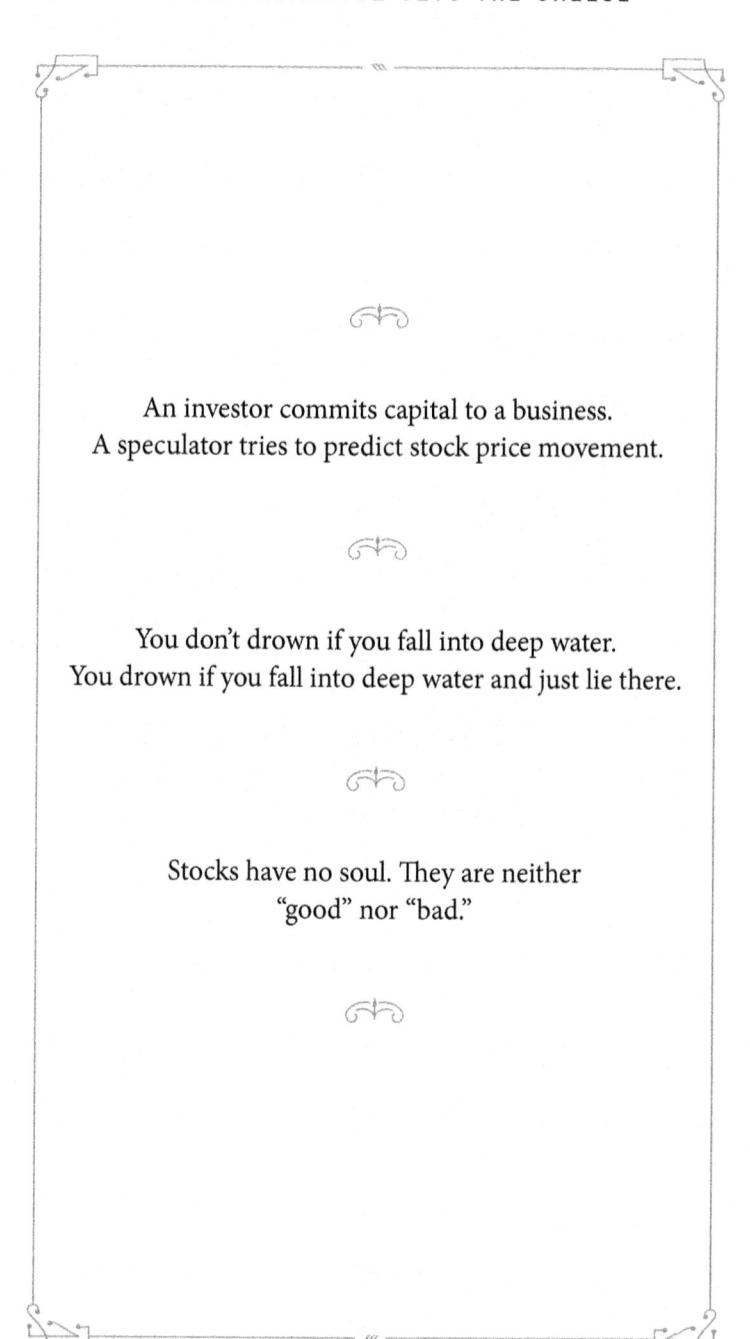

An investor commits capital to a business.
A speculator tries to predict stock price movement.

You don't drown if you fall into deep water.
You drown if you fall into deep water and just lie there.

Stocks have no soul. They are neither
"good" nor "bad."

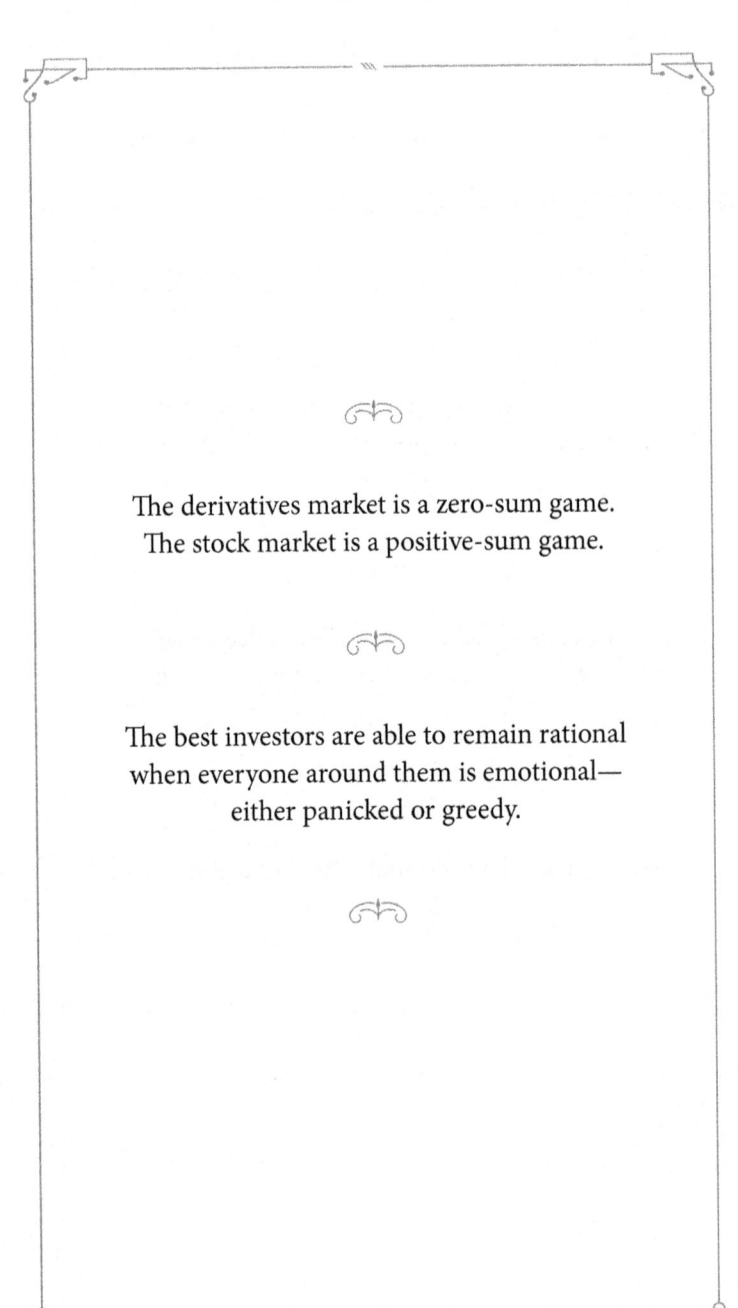

The derivatives market is a zero-sum game.
The stock market is a positive-sum game.

The best investors are able to remain rational when everyone around them is emotional—either panicked or greedy.

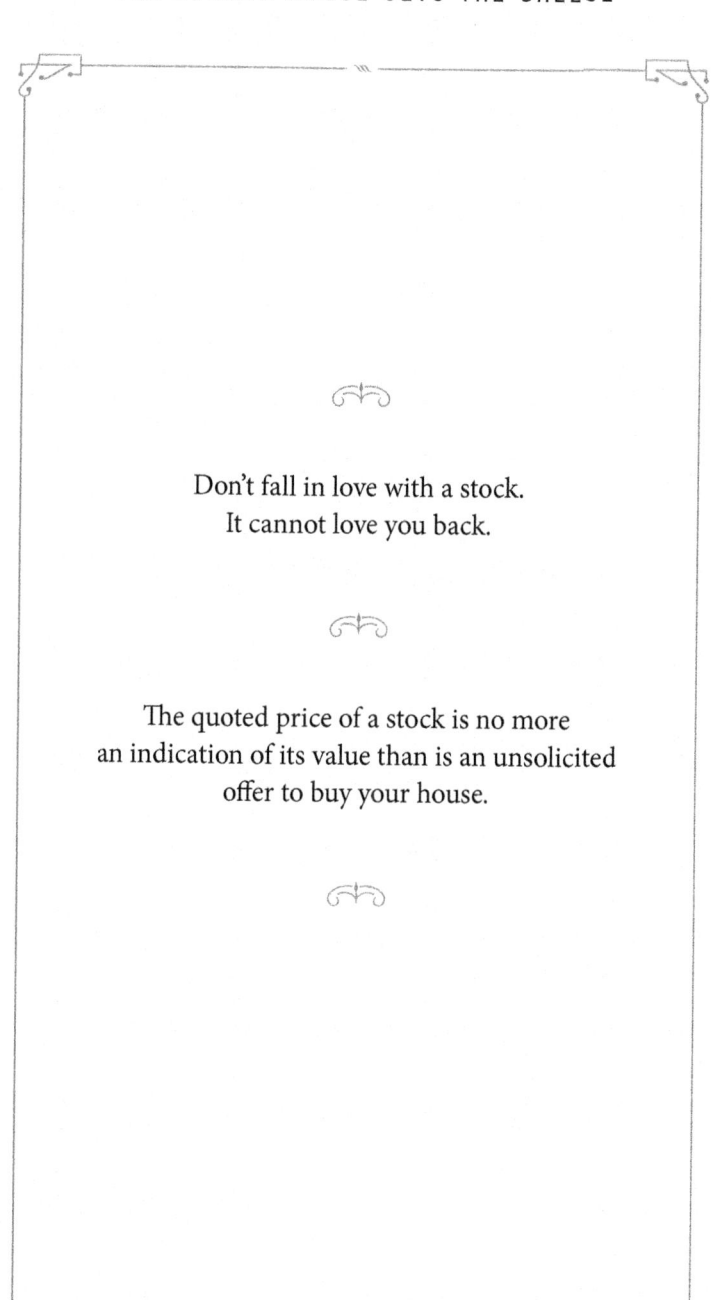

Don't fall in love with a stock.
It cannot love you back.

The quoted price of a stock is no more
an indication of its value than is an unsolicited
offer to buy your house.

The best auctions to attend are those in the rain.

Competition for an asset may reflect its popularity, but as the number of interested buyers for an asset increases, the likelihood of a bargain price declines. The auction sales price of a piece of real estate is determined, among other things, by the number of qualified bidders at the auction—and the number of bidders can be influenced by something as unrelated to the property's value as the weather.

Even though they are protected from precipitation, the trading floors at the New York Stock Exchange were built without windows, so as to insulate traders from the emotional and psychological influences of the weather. However, the lack of windows does nothing to insulate investors from an almost limitless number of other emotional or psychological influences—influences that sometimes artificially decrease or increase the number of investors interested in a stock, thus providing opportunities to investors willing to stand in the rain.

The best investment ideas are often found in the shortest lines.

From 1981 to 2017, the number of people attending the Berkshire Hathaway annual meeting compounded at a faster annualized rate than did the Berkshire Hathaway stock price.

Any action is easier when a lot of others are doing the same thing.

When a stock you are watching or own drops 20%, your first thought should be "why?" not "sell."

THE SECOND MOUSE GETS THE CHEESE

"I DON'T SUPPOSE I COULD GET YOU TO RAISE YOUR BID?"

Great bargains can often be found in doing what is unpopular.

The long-term power of compounding is calculable,
but otherwise almost incomprehensibly awesome.

Your house is not an investment.
It is a place to eat, sleep and shower. If you sell it,
you will have to buy another one.

Gold doesn't do anything. You can't eat it
or even play with it. If you invest in rare wines,
however, when the market collapses at least
you can liquidate your portfolio.

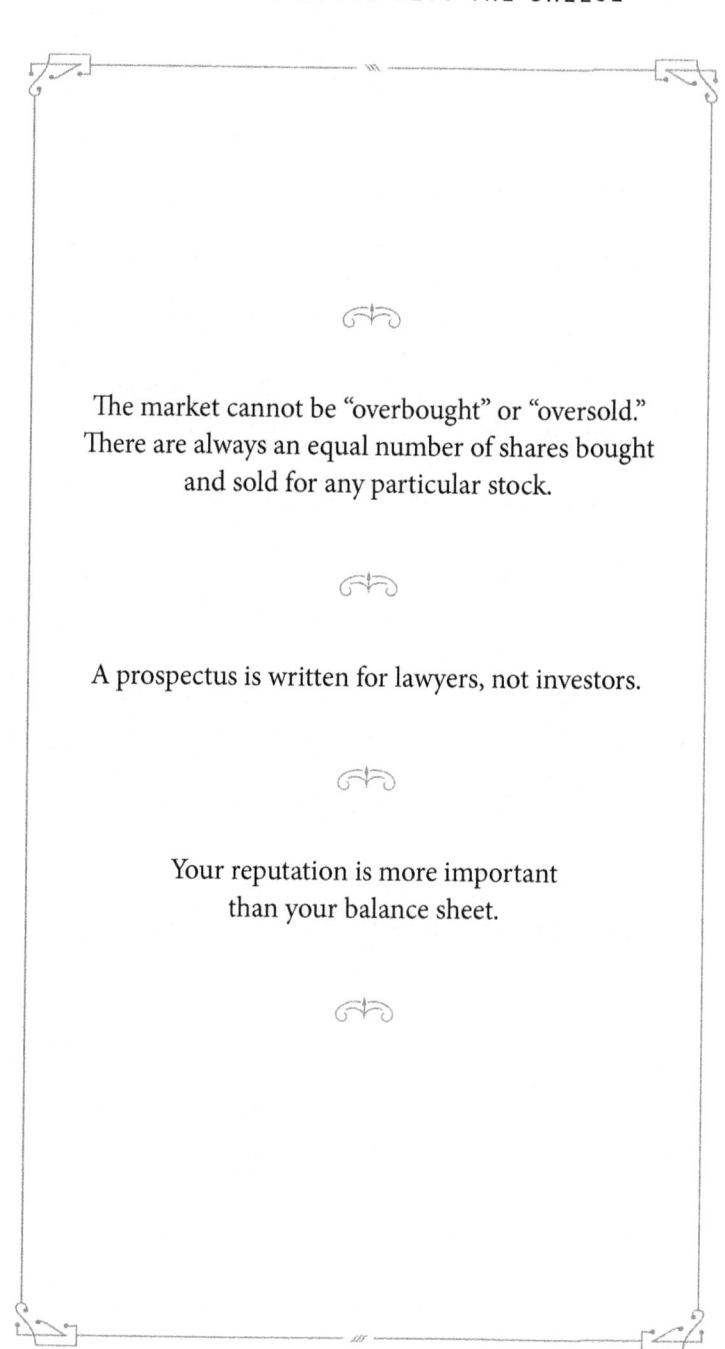

The market cannot be "overbought" or "oversold."
There are always an equal number of shares bought
and sold for any particular stock.

A prospectus is written for lawyers, not investors.

Your reputation is more important
than your balance sheet.

Millions of people sold Wal-Mart stock last week.
About an equal number made and lost money.
The difference?
The price at which they bought the stock.

We only truly see those things on which we focus.

If a stock declines 20% after you buy it, challenge your valuation assumptions. If they are still valid, buy more.

Never use the word "feel" to explain
an investment decision.

There is nothing wrong with buying a stock at
its all-time high price, as long as it is a bargain
relative to its value.

Warren Buffett's words aren't gospel truths.
He is human and fallible—but much less so than
the typical guest on CNBC.

Ignorance is more likely to have killed the cat than curiosity.

The most common investment mistakes result from acting without sufficient understanding or information—that is, ignorance, either of facts or of context.

Berkshire Hathaway Vice Chairman Charlie Munger warns against investors myopically focusing on a single area of life or even business. Instead, he recommends actively building a mosaic of knowledge that serves as a latticework of mental models. Even among the most intelligent people, such a mosaic can only be developed as a result of intentional curiosity.

Great investors are voracious readers of all sorts of material—not just business periodicals or even annual reports. They never miss an opportunity to learn from the people they meet. They choose friends and associates who not only challenge the depth of their thinking, but also expand its breadth.

Who we are and what we accomplish is determined by what we read and the people with whom we choose to associate.

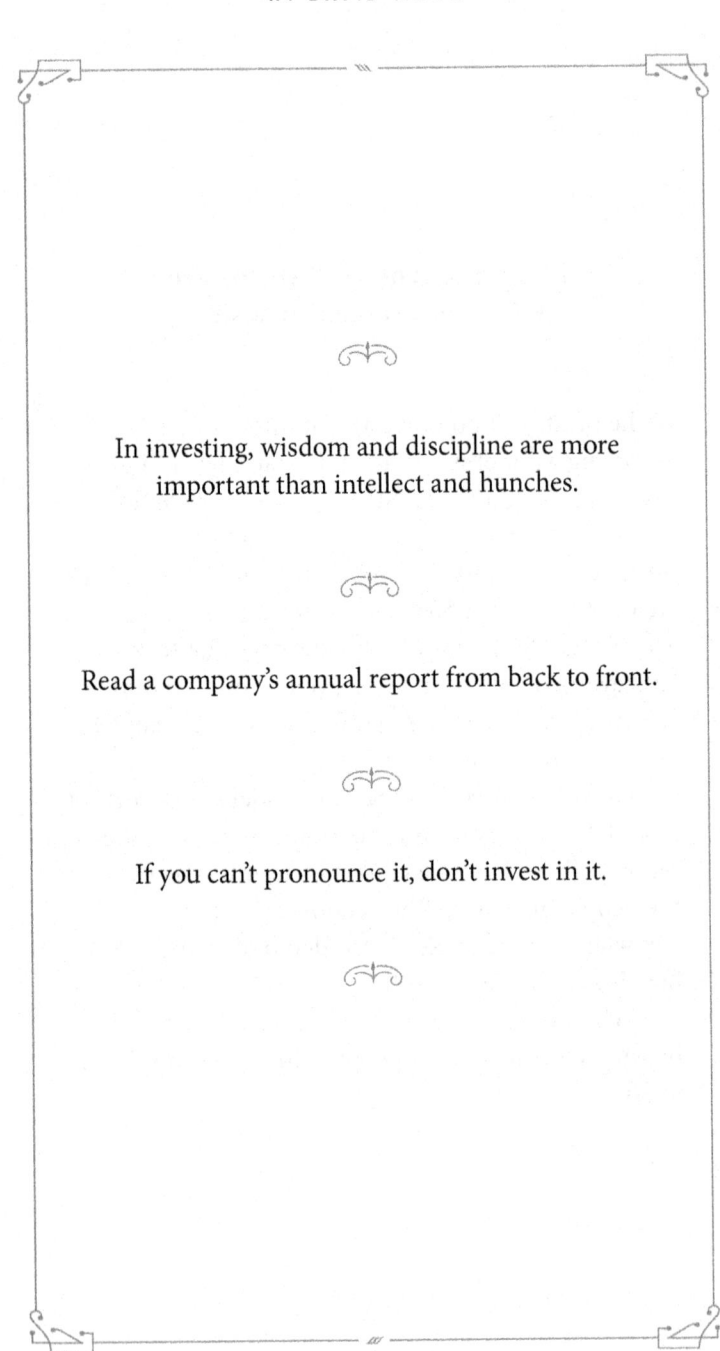

In investing, wisdom and discipline are more important than intellect and hunches.

Read a company's annual report from back to front.

If you can't pronounce it, don't invest in it.

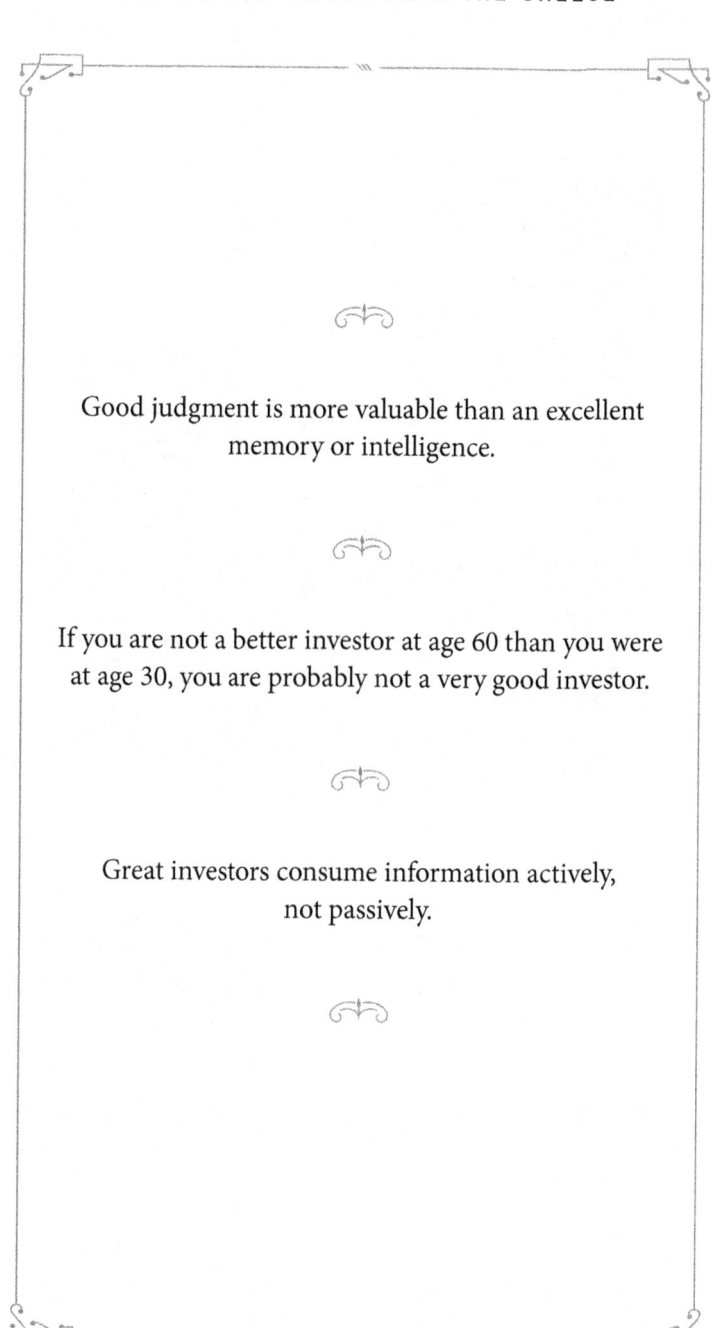

Good judgment is more valuable than an excellent memory or intelligence.

If you are not a better investor at age 60 than you were at age 30, you are probably not a very good investor.

Great investors consume information actively, not passively.

Most people develop their lifelong attitude
about money by the time they are 16.

Being smart and being a smart investor
are not the same thing.

Everyone wants to be a successful investor.
Few are willing to constantly work to improve at it.

The wiser a person is, the luckier he is.

It's no sin to lose money—unless
you learn nothing in the process.

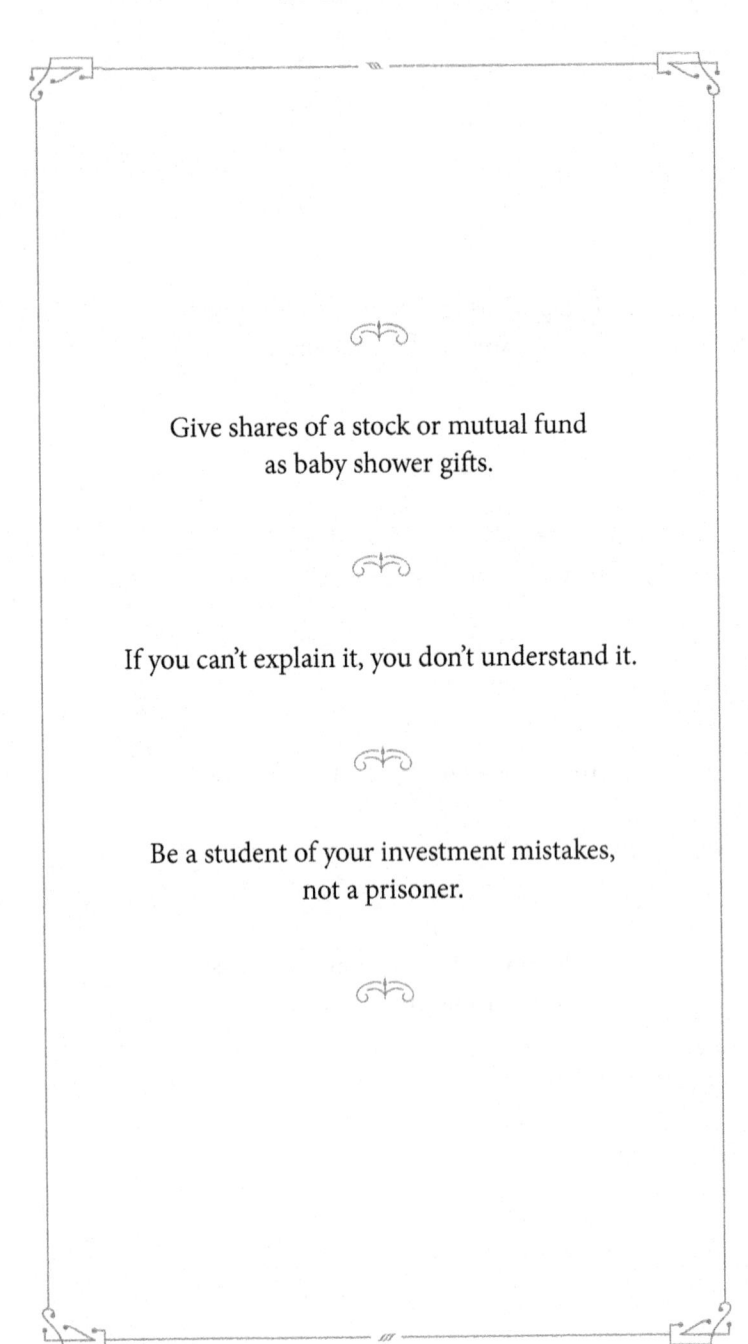

Give shares of a stock or mutual fund
as baby shower gifts.

If you can't explain it, you don't understand it.

Be a student of your investment mistakes,
not a prisoner.

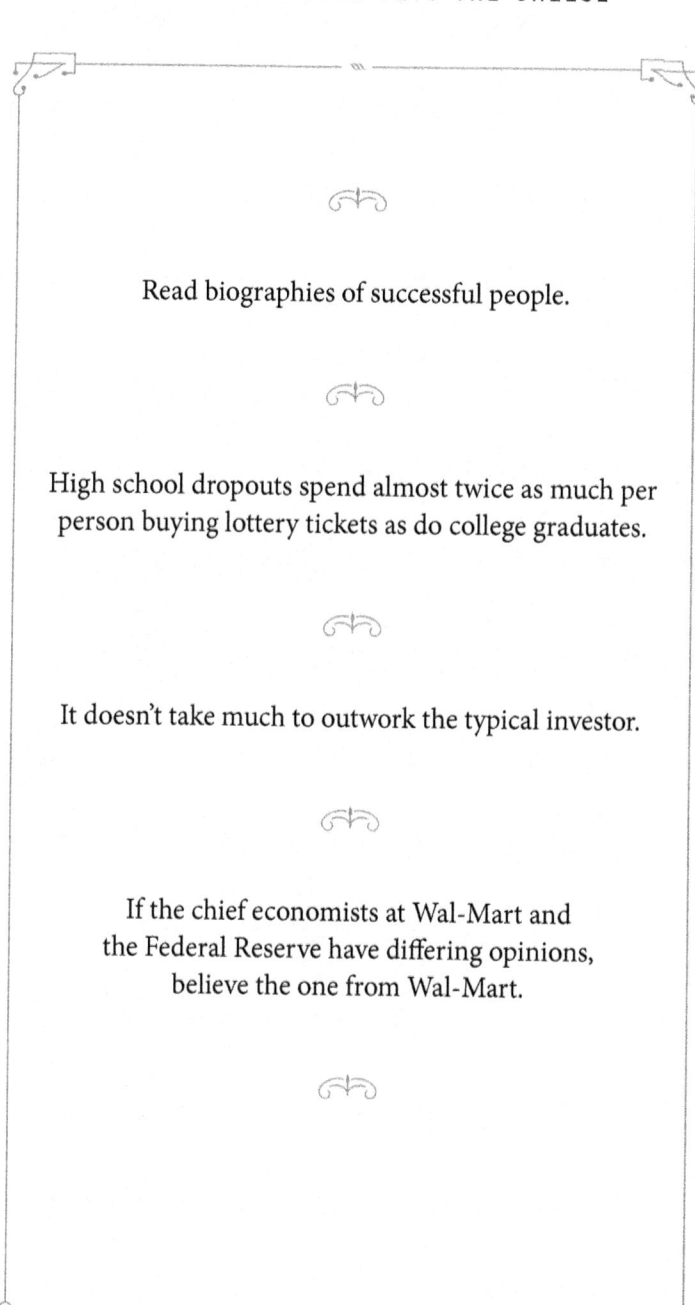

Read biographies of successful people.

High school dropouts spend almost twice as much per person buying lottery tickets as do college graduates.

It doesn't take much to outwork the typical investor.

If the chief economists at Wal-Mart and the Federal Reserve have differing opinions, believe the one from Wal-Mart.

Never name an animal you plan to eat.

In order to get the best possible price when buying an automobile, a buyer must have some degree of indifference about the car he drives. Once he becomes emotionally committed to a particular model, he can no longer walk away. He is almost assured to overpay.

Some people spend decades and tens of thousands of dollars trying to access their feelings. Great investors do the opposite, at least with respect to their investment decisions. The best investors are logical when everyone around them is emotional. Both greed and fear dilute our efforts to reason, sometimes to the point of its complete elimination.

Fear is what causes us to sell following stock price declines. Greed inspires us to buy shares following sharp price increases. Both are emotional recipes for portfolio disaster.

A decision based on logic is easy to change if an underlying assumption is proved to be faulty. A decision based on emotion can only be changed by an even more passionate—that is, illogical—emotion.

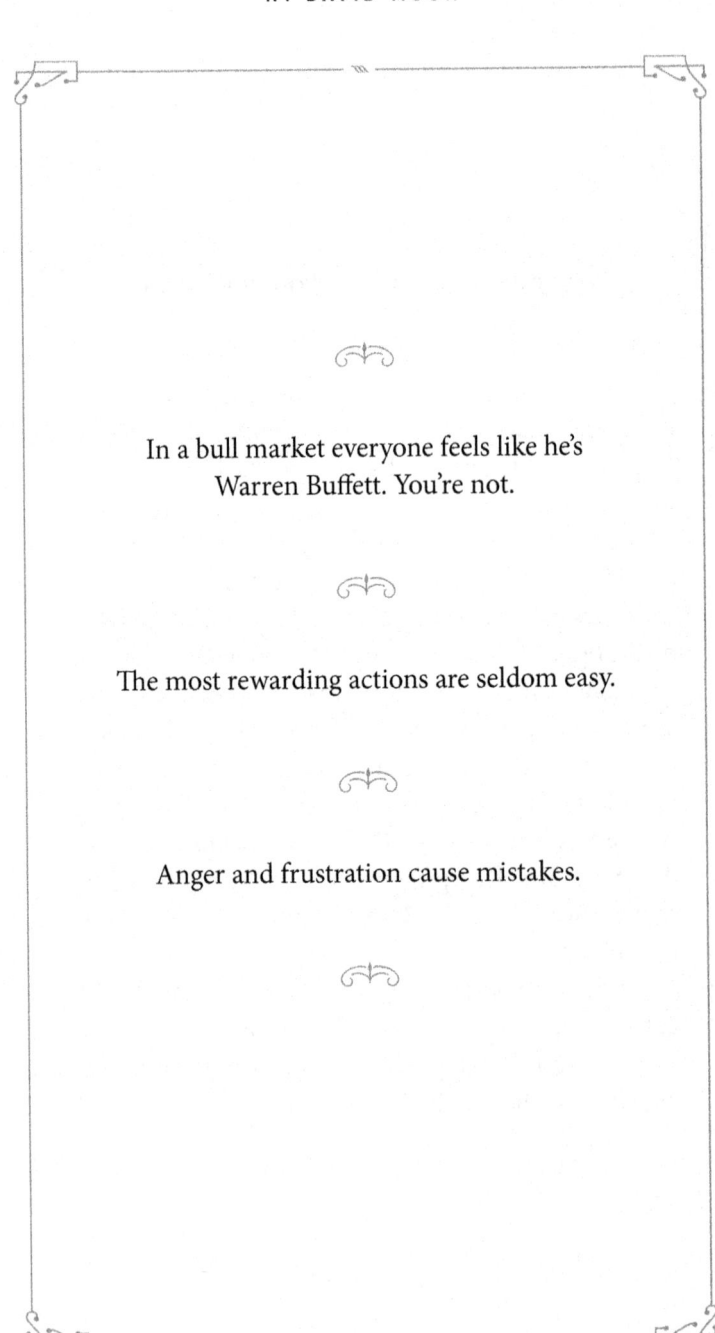

In a bull market everyone feels like he's Warren Buffett. You're not.

The most rewarding actions are seldom easy.

Anger and frustration cause mistakes.

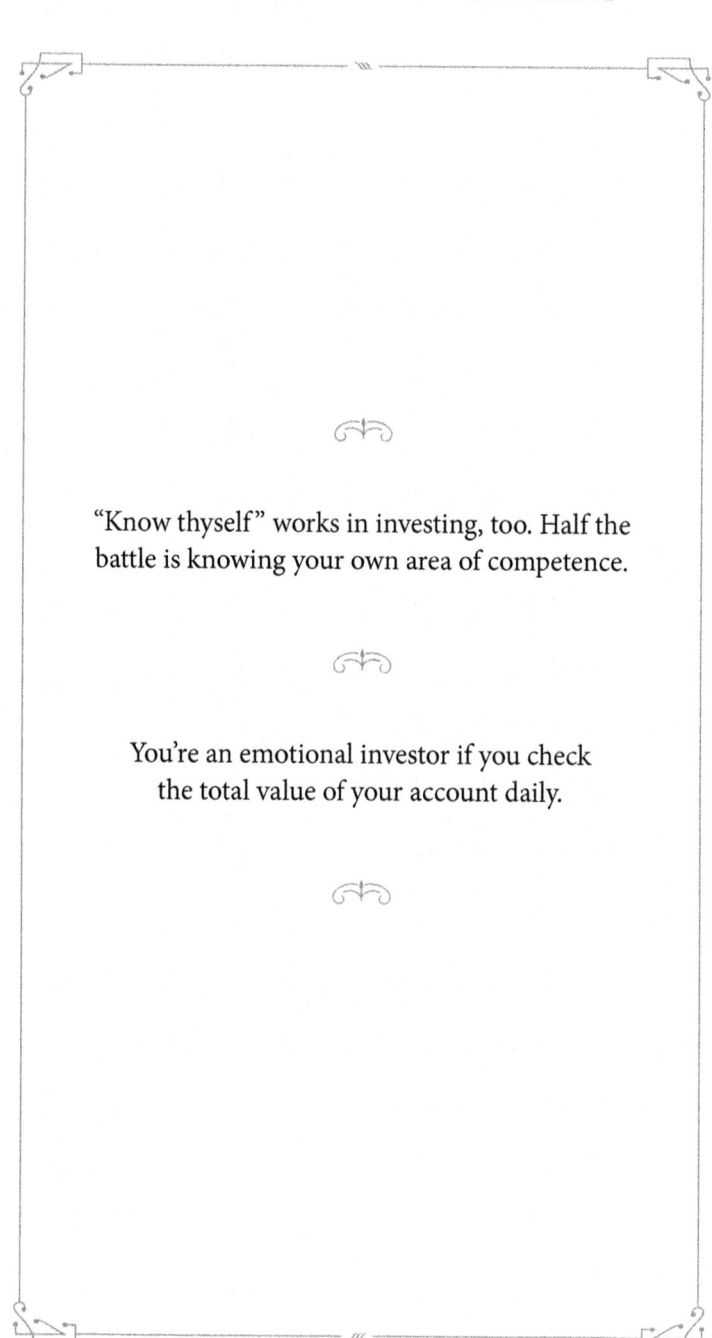

"Know thyself" works in investing, too. Half the battle is knowing your own area of competence.

※

You're an emotional investor if you check the total value of your account daily.

> GLENN REALIZED HE WOULD NEVER FULFILL HIS DREAM OF MAKING HIS OWN SAUSAGE.

As your stress increases, so does your susceptibility to silly suggestions.

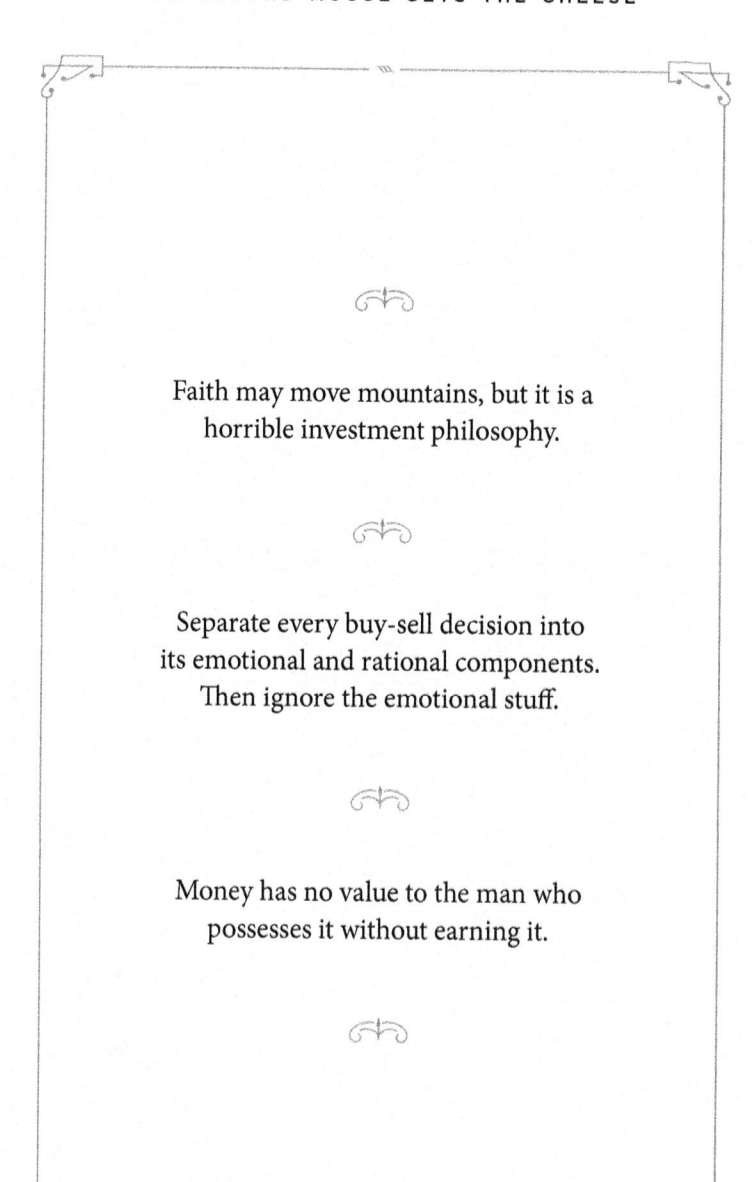

Faith may move mountains, but it is a horrible investment philosophy.

Separate every buy-sell decision into its emotional and rational components. Then ignore the emotional stuff.

Money has no value to the man who possesses it without earning it.

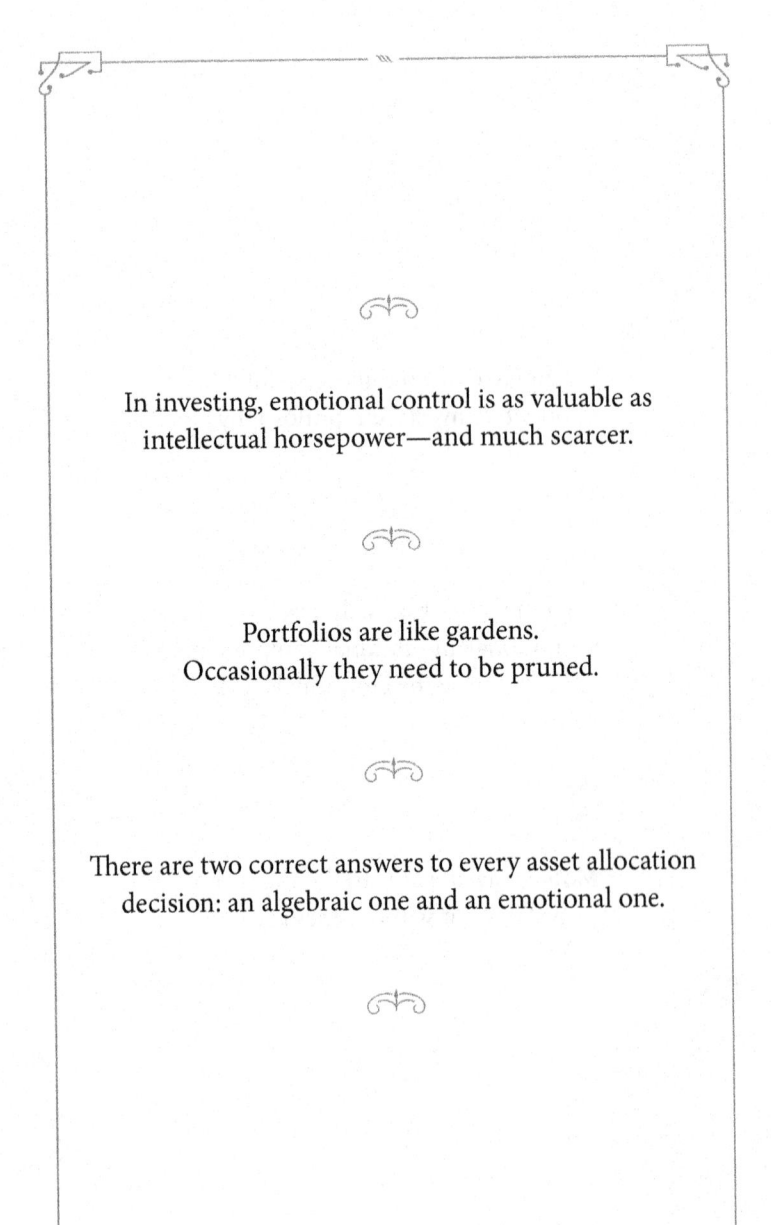

In investing, emotional control is as valuable as intellectual horsepower—and much scarcer.

Portfolios are like gardens. Occasionally they need to be pruned.

There are two correct answers to every asset allocation decision: an algebraic one and an emotional one.

Short attention spans are not useful on Wall Street, in the boardroom or at the dinner table.

Successful investing requires defying the natural tendency to prefer things now—not in the future.

If you have to use the word "hope" to describe a potential investment, do not make that investment.

Postscript

Along with sexuality and spirituality, money is among the most intimate topics in people's lives. Of the three, people are generally more willing to share details of their sex lives and their beliefs about God long before they would consider sharing figures from their tax returns. We develop our relationship with money at an early age and protectively nurture it throughout our lives.

Money is a serious and important subject that some people almost treat with a sense of reverence.

There are a number of traits that great investors share that are sources of great advantage, including intelligence, a strong work ethic, an ability to assess real risk and confidence in their convictions.

This author notwithstanding, however, some of the most accomplished investors also have a keen sense of wit. This does not minimize the serious nature of money in our lives. Great humor and great investing require a similar intent and ability to look at the same things at which other people look, and see things that other people don't see. After laughing at a great joke, we often think to ourselves, "That's so obvious; why didn't I see it that way?"

This unique ability allows great investment analysts and comedians to look well beyond first-order, superficial facts that are obvious to everyone, to discern second-order conclusions that only become obvious to the masses in hindsight. A list of the small number of investors who outperform market averages looks remarkably similar to the list of investors willing to be different and think for themselves. My hope is that these *proverbs for thinking investors* will inspire you to do the same.

> *If you buy the same securities everyone else is buying, you will have the same results as everyone else.*
> —John Templeton

About the Author

W. DAVID MOON is the founder of Moon Capital Management, one of the oldest independent investment research and management firms in East Tennessee. Moon Capital Management provides investment research and portfolio management services to individuals and institutions, in addition to managing a private investment partnership.

David has appeared on CNN and been a regular contributor to CNBC's "After the Bell" segment. His research and editorial writing have been featured in the *Wall Street Journal*, *Barron's* and *Corporate Board Member* magazine. His weekly newspaper column, "MarketView," began distribution in 1996 and is currently carried by the USA TODAY NETWORK.

David is also the author of the award-winning *Thoughts Are Things*, named top Juvenile Inspiration Book of 2014 by the prestigious National Indie Excellence Awards.

His public service has included work with a number of organizations, including the Investment Committee for the City of Knoxville, the UT Graduate School of Medicine Board of Visitors as a charter member and Zoo Knoxville as the Chairman for six years.

For seven years David taught as an adjunct investments professor in the finance department of his alma mater, the University of Tennessee, where he earned a bachelor's degree and MBA (both with Honors) and was an Academic All-Southeastern Conference football selection in 1984.